Women and the U.S. Budget

Jane Midgely says that women are the "shock absorbers"
when essential government services are cut. Due to the impacts
of national policies, they have to be money and budget wizards
at the household level, keeping their families together throughout
economic ups and downs; to add insult to injury, their unpaid work
doesn't show up in any national accounts. *Women and the U.S. Budget*
is a tool to enable ordinary women to insert their values and
common sense into the process of determining how our
public resources are gathered and spent.

— MEIZHU LUI, Executive Director, United for a Fair Economy

If only all the members of Congress and all the TV shouters
would take the time to read this book. *Women and the U.S. Budget*
is an indispensable resource from the woman who pioneered the
"woman's budget" concept. It's for all of us who believe in using
our national funds for social needs, global justice, democracy
and peace. This is a book to have on hand while you read the
newspaper or watch the news, and it's most certainly a book to
bring along when you meet your Congressional representatives!

— MARY DAY KENT, executive director, US Section,
Women's International League for Peace and Freedom

For those who thought it to be impossible, read *Women and the U.S.
Budget* — you'll find an entertaining, clear and engaging
explanation about what is important about our national budget
and tax policy, how it affects women every day, and how US policy
fits into the big picture of world economic growth. Every woman
who wants to give children a good start in life and make this world
a better place to live needs to read this book.

— HEIDI HARTMANN, President, Institute for
Women's Policy Research

WOMEN
and the
U.S. BUDGET

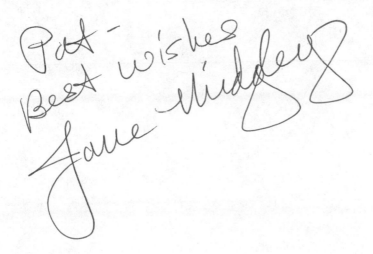

Pat —
Best wishes
Jane Midgley

WOMEN

and the

U.S. BUDGET

Where the Money Goes
and What You Can Do About It

Jane Midgley

NEW SOCIETY PUBLISHERS

To my parents,

Grant and Marsha Midgley

Cataloging in Publication Data:
A catalog record for this publication is available from the National Library
of Canada.

Copyright © 2005 by Jane Midgley.

Cover design by Diane McIntosh. Images: Comstock Images.

Printed in Canada. First printing July 2005.

Paperback ISBN: 0-86571-525-4

To order directly from the publishers, please call toll-free (North America)
1-800-567-6772, or order online at www.newsociety.com

Any other inquiries can be directed by mail to:

New Society Publishers
P.O. Box 189, Gabriola Island, BC V0R 1X0, Canada
1-800-567-6772

New Society Publishers' mission is to publish books that contribute in fundamental ways to building an ecologically sustainable and just society, and
to do so with the least possible impact on the environment, in a manner that
models this vision. We are committed to doing this not just through education, but through action. We are acting on our commitment to the world's
remaining ancient forests by phasing out our paper supply from ancient
forests worldwide. This book is one step toward ending global deforestation
and climate change. It is printed on acid-free paper that is 100% old growth
forest-free (100% post-consumer recycled), processed chlorine free, and
printed with vegetable-based, low-VOC inks. For further information, or to
browse our full list of books and purchase securely, visit our website at:
www.newsociety.com

NEW SOCIETY PUBLISHERS   www.newsociety.com

CONTENTS

❖

ACKNOWLEDGMENTS

❖

THIS BOOK WOULD NOT HAVE BEEN POSSIBLE without the help of many wonderful people who gave me encouragement, provided resources and connections, and read various drafts. Thank you especially to Betty Burkes, Carol Barton, Agnes Williams, Mary Zepernick, Marilyn Rubin, Louise Dunlap, Jan Strout, Judith Nies, Curdina Hill, Susan Moir, Mary Leno, and Donna Cooper. I learned so much from working with George Friday on developing budget literacy for women. A special thank-you to the women who attended the Women's Budget Project national meeting in 1996 (see note 2 in Chapter 8 for more information).

I thank the Women's International League for Peace and Freedom for sending me on this journey to focus on the federal budget and for supporting work on women and budgets. I am also grateful for my year spent at the Bunting Institute at Radcliffe, which gave me space to think more deeply about the issues dealt with in this book.

Special thanks go to my sister, Marty McCune, my brother, John Midgley, and my parents, Grant and Marsha Midgley, who both passed away while I was completing the book. They have always inspired me and believed in me, and that has been the greatest good fortune.

Foreword

❖

At present, our country needs women's idealism and determination, perhaps more in politics than anywhere else.

— Shirley Chisholm

More than 30 years ago, I began my unlikely journey in politics because I was galvanized by the example of a courageous woman. I was a student at Mills College in Oakland, the mother of two small boys, and largely disgusted by what I saw in the world of politics. One of my teachers required all of the students in the class to work on one of the presidential campaigns, and I thought I was going to fail the class because I didn't believe there was a candidate I could believe in enough to support. The woman who saved me from failing that class was Shirley Chisholm, the first African American woman elected to Congress. Her 1972 presidential campaign was a true inspiration to me, and to women everywhere, because she so clearly shattered the myth that there was no space for a woman's perspective in our democracy.

I learned a great deal from Shirley Chisholm over the years, but in considering Jane Midgely's book, one thing stands out the most: Shirley taught me and an entire generation of women and people of color that we could go beyond calling for our rights to be recognized — that we needed to take a seat at the table and exercise those rights.

Women & the U.S. Budget comes at a time when our schools are chronically underfunded, when millions lack basic access to healthcare, and environmental protections that keep safe the air we breathe and the water we drink are under attack. It is a time when we are facing soaring deficits, the massive human and financial costs of an unnecessary war, and a debate about privatizing Social Security, a move that would spell the beginning of the end of our nation's commitment to providing a social safety net to protect the most vulnerable.

It is a time when women need to bring our idealism and determination to the table and play an active role in shaping the priorities that are spelled out in our nation's budget.

I believe that budgets are moral documents. They represent a profound statement of what our nation values. As mothers, daughters, sisters and activists, women are very attuned to the moral implications of the priorities set out in the budget process.

The difficulty with budgets is that they don't lend themselves to a moral reading. Nowhere in the document will it say that increases in Defense spending for new weapons systems, or the extension of tax cuts will be at the expense of funds for housing, food assistance programs or education. But that is indeed what happens.

This book offers an important tool for the difficult task of deciphering both the budget and the process that goes into making it. It is an important tool because it opens up the process, and allows people who aren't policy experts to understand how the budget is made, who makes it and who benefits, and lets them draw their own conclusions about whether the priorities funded in the budget match their own values. Looking at the budget in both a domestic and global context allows us to understand how subtle shifts in funds can translate into significant differences in policy. With a better understanding of the process, we can see more clearly who will be impacted by each decision, and take proactive measures against moves we feel are unjust.

Perhaps more importantly, this book lays the groundwork for looking forward and envisioning a budget that fully reflects our values. It offers a vision of how we can move from a budget that prioritizes tax cuts for the wealthy to one that reflects a commitment to building healthy communities, and that can be measured by investments in creating better-paying jobs, providing access to housing and healthcare, and ensuring that the air we breathe and the water we drink are safe and clean. It offers concrete ways that we can work to move from a budget that prioritizes new weapons systems to one that reflects a commitment to global peace and human rights that can be measured by investments in international diplomacy and measures aimed at addressing poverty, disease and other causes of war and instability. It offers us a blueprint for constructive action to move from a budget that prioritizes subsidies for the oil, coal and nuclear industries to one that reflects our commitment to our future and the planet's future, a commitment that can be measured by investments in our children's education, in renewable and sustainable energy policies and measures to protect our environment.

I love my work, and I have fought to promote women candidates so that there will be more of us in Congress, but you don't need to be an elected official to help restructure our federal priorities. In fact, I believe this sort of change will only come when women in all walks of life begin to get involved and take control of the process of setting our national priorities. No single person can achieve this, but together we can go from just a budget to a budget that is just. As Shirley Chisholm once said, "You must be the change that you want to see in the world."

Congresswoman Barbara Lee is a Co-Chair of the Congressional Progressive Caucus, the Congressional Black Caucus Whip and a Senior Democratic Whip. She serves on the House International Relations Committee and Financial Services Committees, and was first elected to represent California's ninth Congressional District in 1998.

INTRODUCTION

❖

I STARTED WORKING ON THIS BOOK when I was seven years old, although I didn't realize it at the time. My father had just taken a job with a newly elected Democratic senator from Utah, and we moved from Salt Lake City to Washington, DC, to start a new life. While running around the halls of congressional office buildings, listening to debates on the Senate floor, meeting legislators, and helping with re-election campaigns, I was absorbing the rhythms and ways of Washington, DC, with an outsider's sensibility.

I was part of the 1963 Civil Rights March on Washington, joined in the massive anti-war demonstrations during the Vietnam War, became a strong feminist, and worked on housing, racism, and community issues in Washington, DC. With other community activists I challenged the priorities of our city — questioning the presence of JROTC in junior-high schools and military recruiters in the halls of high schools at a time when youth jobs programs and after-school programs were underfunded. I was also one of the organizers of the first Women's Pentagon Action, which brought together peace activists, environmental activists, and a broad range of women's organizations. By that time, I became legislative director (I later served as executive director) of the Women's International League for Peace and Freedom (WILPF) the year Ronald Reagan took over the presidency. I'd had long experience with movements for positive social change that had an alternative vision for the United States.

In the early 1980s I watched David Stockman, the president's budget director, make deep cuts in spending for human needs without public knowledge or debate, and I heard Richard Perle advocate an expensive new generation of nuclear weapons that put the world on a hair trigger. The national budget was being distorted by ideologues, with the help of many men and women in Congress. To counter this, WILPF participated in national coalitions calling for new budget priorities and organized training sessions to teach women about the federal budget. Later, after publishing the Women's Budget — a proposal for cutting 50 percent of the military budget and investing it in social programs — we held citizens' hearings in cities around the country, bringing women together to highlight the impact of national and state budget and economic policies on women and children.

My international travels took me to the groundbreaking 1995 United Nations Fourth World Conference on Women in Beijing, China. This historic meeting set a comprehensive global agenda for women's advancement. At that time I founded the Women's Budget Project, bringing women activists and economists together to analyze current budget and economic policies and develop an alternative framework. The work on budgets and gender issues has exploded around the world ever since the Beijing meeting. I hope this book can help move this work forward in the United States.

In *Women and the US Budget*, I invite the reader to take on the role of a public investigator (or PI). A PI in this case scrutinizes the shadowy areas of the public realm to see what is really going on and to break through the secrecy surrounding how our public resources are gathered and spent. A PI's strategy is to make visible what has been invisible — to make understandable what has been mysterious. The budget and the budget process are shrouded in mystery for all but a few experts, and a lack of openness in this area represents a major roadblock to achieving our ideal of democracy. Once the budget is transparent — once the reality behind it is visible — it loses its power to overwhelm us or keep us at a distance. We can approach it and choose our response.

The national budget represents the resources of the people of the United States. The budget is drawn up by the Congress and the president, but the money does not belong to them. It belongs to all of us. We can forget that these are our resources they are collecting and dividing up, either because we feel too removed from the budgeting process or because we have lost hope in the political system. Even if we have awareness that these are our resources, we often feel power-less to create change.

For Parts One and Two of *Women and the US Budget: Where the Money Goes and What You Can Do About It*, pretend you are a PI try-ing to solve the mystery of how the budget affects women and their families. In Part One you will investigate the basics of the federal budget — where the money comes from, where it goes, whether the budget is balanced or runs a surplus or deficit, and who decides. In Part Two, you will look at how the budget interacts with the US economy and the global economy. In Part Three, you will think about principles, values, and a structure for a new budget, and you will learn about strategies and resources you can use to take action on the budget and economic policies.

As a PI, you can draw inspiration from fictional female sleuths like Blanche White, V.I. Warshawski, Anna Pigeon, and Nancy Drew, the creations of BarbaraNeely, Sara Paretsky, Nevada Barr, and Mildred Wirt Benson (aka Carolyn Keene). These characters use a combination of persistence, love, intuitive knowledge, keen powers of observation, and courageous action.

Blanche White is fiercely independent and self-sufficient and also acutely aware of the politics of race, class, and gender. She has to nav-igate them with skill to secure her own well-being and that of her children and her community. V.I. Warshawski is keenly tuned in to the class politics of Chicago and is not afraid to go up against the powerful political forces that want to stifle the truth and maintain the status quo. Anna Pigeon, a park ranger, is powerfully connected to nature and wilderness and is determined to uncover the facts no mat-ter what danger or violence she herself experiences. Nancy Drew uses her upper-class influence when needed, dressing up and conforming to help her get information, but she will go anywhere and do any-thing to solve a mystery and see justice served.

All of these characters are masters at using logic and tapping into their intuition. It's safe to say that without their advanced access to deep knowing (the ability to know something without knowing why you know), they would have been dead many times over. They show PIs how to integrate intuition, emotion, and reason.

PI Pointers throughout Parts One and Two will help you dig below the surface of the budget. There are also exercises and questions in Chapter 9 to help you explore the connection between the national budget, your personal budget, and your life, and to help you determine actions you may want to take.

CHAPTER 1

❖

Women and Abundance

> There exists an obligation toward every human being
> for the sole reason that he or she is a human being,
> without any other condition requiring to be fulfilled
> .... This obligation is an eternal one .... This obligation
> is an unconditional one.
>
> — Simone Weil, *The Need for Roots*

IN THE UNITED STATES TODAY we are surrounded by an abundance of economic resources that should insure everyone has adequate food, healthcare, housing, education, and jobs at good wages. Instead we find ourselves falling far short of providing those basic needs for all our people. The economic resources we do have as a country represent the labor — paid and unpaid — of everyone in the United States. As workers, taxpayers, and nurturers within our families and communities, women are major contributors to this abundance. But do we understand the depth of our contribution? Are we in a position to tap into our current economic abundance for the good of our families, our communities, and ourselves? Can we envision a society in which everyone has access to that abundance?

Economic abundance includes three things: income, wealth, and assets. Income is financial gain that comes to a person in a given period of time from, for example, salary, self-employment or small business income, interest from investments, or gifts. Wealth is an accumulation of money that is held in bank accounts, stocks, and other financial instruments. Assets can include some of the elements of wealth, but assets are also things like land and buildings a person

owns, other material possessions, and rights to future pension payments. In order to calculate the actual wealth and assets of a person, business, or country, liabilities (debts owed to others) have to
be subtracted.

A budget is a forecast of what money will be accumulated and
how it will be spent over a specific period of time. It is used to set priorities as well as to monitor what actually happens. For example, if
you wanted to do a budget for your household for a month, you
would include all the sources of income you expect for that month as
well as all the things you need and want to buy.

The US budget sets out the government's plan for the coming year,
as well as recording the receipts and spending of previous years. The
process of planning a budget includes making decisions on how to
use other government resources beyond simply revenues and expenditures, just as your personal finances involve more than just your
monthly income and expenses. The government's other resources
include debt, savings, investments, and assets.

The national budget is a window on the larger patterns of how
our common resources are used, and the aim of *Women and the
US Budget* is to provide "budget literacy" so we can better understand
and influence the management of those resources. The US national
budget is vast and has a powerful impact on communities across the
United States and around the world. Federal government spending
makes up a large portion of the nation's economy — almost 18 percent of the total goods and services produced — and the government
exerts a strong influence on economic trends and the political and
social well-being of the nation through taxation and spending policy.

Every woman's life is inextricably connected to what happens in
Washington, no matter what her race, class, ethnicity, job, or family
situation. From CEO subsidies to summer youth programs, food
stamps to school lunches, Social Security checks to home mortgage
deductions, a visit to the Grand Canyon to a drink of water from the
tap, the budget decisions of the government affect women's lives on
a daily basis. In spite of this, and in spite of the fact that women are
full participants in the economy as workers and taxpayers and com-
prise over half of the population, they make up only 13 percent of the
members of the US Congress. This means our voices are not being
fully heard, and our experiences and wisdom are mostly left out

when important decisions are made. It also means that when the budget pie is being cut up, women and the families they support, alone or with a partner, can end up with the smallest slice.

In recent years, women, especially women of color, have been singled out and criticized for relying on national programs in the budget, and these criticisms have been used to justify cutbacks in welfare and housing subsidies. For instance, during the 1990s, advocates of reforming welfare argued that Aid to Families with Dependent Children (AFDC) was breaking the budget when it actually took just one percent of it. They promoted an image of welfare abusers — usually African American women, although only 40 percent of the recipients were African Americans — who received aid for many years. Most women on AFDC were women supporting one or two young children on their own and who needed transitional help to get back on their feet after a financial setback. The average time spent on welfare was only a few years.

In fact, all sectors of society depend on help from the government for housing (think home mortgage interest deduction), retirement money (Social Security), physical infrastructure (such as highways), healthcare (Medicare and Medicaid), and many other services, provided by our national pooled resources. In addition, the unpaid and unrecognized work that women do in their homes and communities is the foundation for the productivity of the "official" economy and deeply affects national priorities as reflected in the budget. It is estimated that the value of unpaid elder care, for instance, is $257 billion annually, and that women are 6 out of 10 of the unpaid caregivers. If women did not provide this care, more public resources would need to be invested in paying for home health services, or longer hospital and institutional care. A Rice University study found that some caregivers lost substantial work time and experienced a reduction of more than $10,000 in annual earnings. Women who cared for elderly parents were more likely to end up in poverty themselves than women who did not provide care.

Women have made strides in labor force participation and therefore in contributions to their families' financial well-being, and they make enormous unpaid contributions, yet they are not always rewarded by the economy.

❖ According to the Government Accountability Office (GAO) (formerly the General Accounting Office), the pay gap between men and women persists. Between 1983 and 2000, women earned approximately 44 percent less than men, 20 percent less after adjusting for experience, education, and occupation. Since 2000 that gap has widened, with women making 75 cents for every dollar a man earns.

❖ In the area of wealth and assets, women on the whole are also behind. There are no studies on the real distribution of wealth between men and women (information is collected by household), but there are indications that men still dominate wealth ownership, particularly of income-producing assets. Women of color are even more challenged in this area. According to a report by Rakesh Kochhar for the Pew Hispanic Center, whites enjoy an 11 to 1 wealth advantage over Hispanics, and a 14 to 1 wealth advantage over blacks.

❖ Most women who do work have no pension, which endangers their quality of life when they stop working or if they separate from their partner or spouse.

The US budget affects all these aspects of women's economic lives. It is one tool that could help meet the needs of all US citizens, but we have yet to agree as a country that all people, including women, have a right to food, shelter, jobs, healthcare, and education. Until we do, the national budget will continue to be a central arena for this debate about the role of government.

The budget, and money itself, are not inherently bad or good. The way in which a government accumulates and spends money determines whether it will be a force for good or a force for injustice. In the same way, there is nothing inherently bad or good about governments, nor is government inherently inefficient. In a democracy, ideally everyone would be involved in determining the government's priorities, yet we currently have a system that discourages many from participating.

Decisions about what the United States spends its money on should flow from clarity about the country's mission and clarity about the strategies needed to fulfill that mission. As a country, we should share in a vision for ourselves, answering the questions:

❖ What are the core values we share and want to embody in how we collect and use our resources?

❖ What can the government provide that can't be provided effectively in any other way?

It is crucial that women in the United States join across class and race lines to take a stronger part in determining the answers to these questions. I wrote *Women and the US Budget* to encourage more engagement with these issues, and in Part Three we will look at values and principles that could guide the distribution of public resources in order to provide a better quality of life for all of us.

The Bigger Picture

The tragic events of September 11, 2001, and their aftermath changed the dynamics around the US national budget, just as they changed so much else. The president's and Congress's response to the attacks on the World Trade Center and the Pentagon revealed that the United States has abundant national resources. Within days, the federal government made $40 billion available for disaster relief to New York City, emergency relief to victims' families, and increased security.

Where did that money come from? The fact that the resources could be made available so quickly illustrates that although the budget is a plan for how money will be raised and spent in a given time period, it is also flexible enough to respond to unexpected events and changed circumstances. This is a positive thing. It would be absurd if, in a budget of over $2 trillion, money could not be found to address the national needs after September 11.

It is a good idea to look deeper, however, if we are to understand the complex maneuvering that happens when so many resources are at stake. September 11 demanded a quick response from the government, but a quick response cannot take all relevant factors into account. A quick response also tends to favor those with ongoing access to decision makers. So, for example, an airline assistance act was passed a few weeks after September 11, giving $5 billion to the airlines immediately, and slated to cost $17 billion over five years. This act became law at a time when thousands of workers in the airline industry and other industries were being laid off, yet the aid was not tied to retaining workers or limiting CEO salaries and benefits.

Another example of the shortsightedness inherent in a quick national response is provided by the dilemmas faced by states in their budgeting after September 11. As the federal government rearranged the flow of money, it chose not to help states with their fiscal crises. Before September 11, states were already facing challenges. Because of the ongoing recession, they were receiving less income (unemployed workers can't pay taxes), and were dealing with more human needs (for instance many women who got off welfare to take a job were losing their jobs). September 11 also created a lot of new expenses as states and local communities had to beef up security. The national government faced all these things, too, but the difference was, as State Senator Sue Tucker of Massachusetts said, "States can't print money. We have to balance our budgets."[1] Massachusetts — the state in which I live — faced a $1 billion deficit and began to slash programs such as higher education, homecare, substance abuse treatment, and instruction in English as a second language.

When expenditures increase during an emergency, it is time to look at the tax side of a budget. There is an option to postpone or repeal tax cuts that have already been passed, or to increase taxes to cover the new expenses. However, the federal government and many states did the opposite in the last months of 2001. They continued to limit income to the system — by refusing to raise taxes — when the need for money to cover expenses was higher. The result was that those people with the least influence in the political process were more likely to see their programs cut so the budget could be balanced.

Because the federal government can issue money, it can sustain a deficit budget. Deficit spending can be a positive thing if it is used to provide needed services and programs in a year when revenues may be short, and it can help stimulate the economy when times are hard. But if deficits are allowed to get too big or to accumulate year after year, the results are higher interest costs to taxpayers and the investment of more of our national resources into paying off the national debt. As we will see in Chapter 4, when deficits are high, bondholders and investors make money, while more of the taxes paid by average taxpayers go to cover interest payments.

Since September 11, 2001, the amount of money in the US budget going to the military and to security agencies for the war on terrorism has increased and will stay high for many years to come. President George W. Bush requested an increase of close to $50 billion in his fiscal year 2003 budget, which was the third-largest increase in military spending in a single year (after the increases for 1952 and 1966). In addition, the military budget is still loaded with expensive aircraft, submarines, ships, and other weapons that were originally designed to fight the Soviet Union. This money, which goes to military contractors to develop, build, and maintain these weapons, does more to protect military contractor profits than it does to protect anyone from terrorism.

Many members of the American armed forces and many Iraqis have been killed or injured in the war. In addition to the grief, pain, and stress this has brought to service people and their families and to so many Iraqis, the increased military expenses put a strain on the national budget and the resources available to address domestic needs. Typically, wars have had the effect of holding steady or reducing spending on social programs within the United States, and this is happening again. Over $150 billion has been spent on the war and the US presence in Iraq so far, and additional expenditures — over $80 billion as of the end of 2004 — are on the way. However, a CBS News/*New York Times* poll in January 2005 found that 57 percent of adults disapprove of the way President Bush is handling the war in Iraq. If the war becomes increasingly unpopular, public opinion could challenge the scenario of continually escalating costs and casualties.

We can't use terrorism as an excuse for neglecting the human needs of our own people. The events of September 11 have understandably made everyone in the United States acutely aware of national security, and we do need to address legitimate security weaknesses that make people vulnerable to harm. Yet President George W. Bush's response to terrorism directed against the United States has eroded our civil liberties and increased economic and social pressure on immigrants and people of color in general. True national security comes from a strong democracy and internal well-being. Unless we have distributed our resources well and insured that all families and children have adequate income, enough to eat, and decent housing, we are undermining what we want to protect.

It is illuminating to look at women's perspectives on domestic priorities. In a survey conducted for the Business and Professional

Women's Foundation by the Institute for Women's Policy Research in 2004, nearly nine out of ten women (86 percent) said that healthcare costs were of major importance, while just under half (49 percent) said homeland security was the most important issue. Homeland security ranked well behind retirement security (80 percent), job opportunities (71 percent), good schools (66 percent), and housing costs (61 percent) in a list of issues. Domestic security is important but not the most important thing, while issues of adequate healthcare coverage and retirement income are at the top of the list. These are issues that the national budget can more fully address on behalf of women and families.

Women and Work

Although women in the United States have made tremendous gains in recent decades in terms of their access to education and the labor market, many women still face a triple burden in the US economy. First, women are concentrated in lower-paying jobs with fewer benefits. Second, women are often the unpaid caregivers in US society, bearing children and providing primary care for them and for the family generally, which often includes caring for elderly parents. They usually do not receive money for doing this work, which is not counted as a productive contribution to the economy and which can interfere with their full-time participation in the labor force. Third, when women do not have enough income to support themselves and their children, they are often given inadequate support by the government or are refused assistance from public resources. This triple bind is worse for poor women and women of color due to the added effects of discrimination based on race and class.

Even as women in the 21st century enjoy a greater share of the economic pie than they have had in the past, racism and classism continue to block progress for certain groups of women. Teresa L. Amott and Julie Matthaei look into the histories of these groups, and their relationships to the US economic system and government, in their book *Race, Gender and Work: A Multi-Cultural Economic History of Women in the United States*. A brief overview of these histories and conditions show:

❖ Native American women have increased their workforce

participation in the last 20 years, but their community still suffers from high unemployment and underemployment.

❖ African American women have also increased their labor force participation but are still concentrated in lower-paying jobs, and their community suffers persistent cycles of poverty.

❖ Chicana labor force participation rates have risen, but Chicanas still remain concentrated in low-paid, seasonal jobs and suffer high poverty rates.

❖ Puerto Rican women in the United States have experienced an increase in labor force participation in recent years, but the gains tend to be less than those of other groups.

❖ Many Chinese American women have been subjected to sweatshop conditions, sewing either in their own homes or in sweatshop factories. Some have become unionized through UNITE (Union of Needletrades, Industrial and Textile Employees, now joined with the Hotel Employees and Restaurant Employees International Union).

❖ Japanese American women have labor participation rates similar to European American women, but their earnings are far less than those of Japanese American men.

❖ Although European American women have made great progress in moving into upper-tier management and professional jobs, they still tend to be underpaid, and most continue in lower-paying jobs.

More women have entered the job market in recent years, and their overall wages have been increasing. However, in a 2004 press release from the Institute for Women's Policy Research, Dr. Heidi Hartmann, president of the institute, reported that "women continue to take a major hit in the on-going economic slowdown. No progress on the wage ratio has been made since 2001, and women actually lost ground in 2004. Falling real wages for women indicate a decline in the quality of their jobs. The economic recovery continues to disadvantage women by failing to provide strong job growth at all wage levels."

Most new jobs that will be available for women in the coming years pay low annual wages that keep women in the ranks of the working poor. According to the Self-Sufficiency Standard for Massachusetts, developed by a coalition of organizations in 1999 headed by the Women's Educational and Industrial Union in Boston, a family of one adult and two children (one of preschool age) in Boston needs over $45,865 a year to provide the basics of life. This is vastly more than most women are able to make as single parents.

Women supporting children on their own are more likely to be poor because of the low pay available to women — especially those with little education and few job skills — and the lack of affordable, high-quality daycare. According to the Joint Center for Political and Economic Studies, the median income for families headed by a single white woman with children in 2001 was $30,062, compared to $63,862 for white married couples. The median income for families maintained by black single mothers was $20,894, compared to $51,514 for black married couples.

Although the official unemployment rate is 5.4 percent, if you include people who want work but have stopped looking and "contingent workers" — part-time, temporary, and contract workers — between a quarter and a third of the US labor force is unemployed or underemployed. Women make up more than two thirds of part-time workers and over half of those who would prefer to work full-time. Part-time contingent workers earn only 60 percent as much as full-time workers on an hourly basis, are not protected under occupational health and safety regulations, and do not receive unemployment insurance. In addition, few part-time workers have employer-provided health insurance. Many workers who are able to find full-time work have found that their wages do not lift them out of poverty.

There are several government policies, in addition to direct income subsidies like housing and food stamps, that affect jobs and wages for women. These include minimum wage and other wage policies, pay equity regulations and enforcement, labor policy, pension policy, Occupational Safety and Health Administration (OSHA) enforcement, affirmative action, and funding for childcare, healthcare, and other basic supports. Government labor policy also has a strong impact on women's economic security. Union women earn more than their nonunion counterparts, and receive better benefits. When the US government contributes to a weakening of labor unions, as the Reagan presidency did in 1981 when it decertified the air traffic controllers' union, all workers are affected.

The federal minimum wage remains at $5.15 an hour, a ridiculously low amount by any standard. A worker who works full-time at this wage earns less than $10,000 a year. Women, especially African American and Hispanic women, would reap the rewards of any minimum-wage increase — they make up 61 percent of the group of workers at the bottom of the income scale.

One goal of national economic public policy should be to insure that women have the training and opportunities to achieve economic autonomy. This means freedom to follow the life path of their choice, enjoying a reasonable standard of living, with or without a male partner. It also means freedom from domestic violence. Most women who leave violent husbands or partners, especially if they take their children with them, end up in poverty for at least a period of time.

Privatization, Entitlements, and Women

In recent decades there has been a strong trend to privatize government services. This means that services previously provided by the national, state, or local governments are taken over by corporations or, in some cases, nonprofit organizations. The corporations that take over the contracts are paid public money, but provide the service as part of a profit-making enterprise. One example of privatization is the use of corporations to fight the war in Iraq — as security guards, supply workers, weapons handlers and to provide support services to the troops. Currently 10 percent of US military personnel work for private contractors. Another example of privatization is the move to hand off welfare reform implementation, child support enforcement, and data collection to Lockheed Martin, which has branched out from military contracts.

When government services are privatized, public sector jobs are lost, and the jobs created by private companies don't generally replace the wages and benefits of the lost jobs. Also, government can provide services such as low-income housing, which may not be profitable for the private sector to undertake. When government decides not to provide those types of services, they may disappear altogether.

This movement of public money into the hands of private companies is a central concern for women. According to "Why Privatizing Government Services Would Hurt Women Workers," a 2003 study by the Institute for Women's Policy Research, most public sector jobs are held by women. Because public sector employees are unionized, they generally have higher wages and better access to employer-funded health insurance and pension benefits than do workers in the private sector. Women's wages are closer to men's wages in the public sector than in the private sector. These are key issues for women's economic security. African American women hold the highest number, proportionately, of public sector jobs, so they are disproportionately hurt when these jobs are eliminated.

Besides eliminating public sector jobs, the move to privatization is threatening three key programs for women: Social Security, Medicare, and Medicaid. The importance of these programs to women is partly due to the fact that because women earn less overall in the job market, and because the United States does not have national health insurance, they rely more on the government for support when they need healthcare for themselves or their children, or when they have retired. For instance, most women receive very low monthly benefits from Social Security, yet the Social Security Administration reports that for one third of women over 65, it is their only income. However, these facts are not usually considered when Congress debates these programs, nor are they taken into account when reform proposals are made.

The Social Security Case Study

To help us understand the move to privatization, we can look at Social Security as a case study. Social Security is the jewel of federal government programs. It has benefited more people than any other government program in US history, enjoys broad political support, and promotes social solidarity. This retirement, disability, and survivor insurance program serves 43 million people a year, yet is very efficient, with only 0.8 percent of income going to pay for administration. Most importantly, it has radically reduced poverty for the elderly.

The campaign to privatize Social Security is taking place in the context of some legitimate questions about the long-term financing of social security that need to be debated in the public arena and addressed by Congress. The Social Security Trustees reported in 2003 that if no reform takes place, Social Security would be able to pay full benefits only until 2042. At that point the trust funds would be depleted, but incoming tax revenue could still cover more than 70 percent of promised benefits. The challenge is that as the baby boomers retire, there has to be enough cash to pay out benefits each year. Many people are worried that there will not be enough money available to cover everyone as early as 2018.

There are many proposals for addressing the long-term needs of the Social Security program without resorting to private accounts. At a press conference on Social Security privatization held by the National Council of Women's Organizations in February 2005, Kim Gandy, president of NOW, recommended two strategies for assuring Social Security's fiscal soundness as well as its ability to provide more equity in benefits for women. The first was a modest increase in the payroll tax around the year 2020, and the second involved raising the income level at which taxes are paid into the system.

However, the President's Council of Economic Advisers argues that workers should be allowed to divert money from Social Security and put it into private savings accounts that they could invest in the stock market. Under one proposal, they could put 4 percent of their earnings, up to $1,000 per year, into an individual account. This leaves these individual accounts vulnerable to the vagaries of the stock market and also takes money out of the Social Security system that will be needed to pay benefits to those retiring in any given year. This is the foot in the door of privatization — and it is not necessary to insure the continuation of Social Security. It is estimated that the cost of shifting to a system of individual accounts could add as much as $4.7 trillion to the national debt over four decades.

If the Social Security system is not broke, as politicians and pundits claim, why are we having a national debate about whether or not we should privatize it? The reason is hidden in the perverse dictates of globalization. The "needs" of banks, bond traders, mutual fund companies, and insurance companies to make ever-increasing profits in the casino of the international economy has caused them to set their sights on public money. The Social Security funds of the United States are one of the largest pools of public money in the world, and they are vulnerable to being raided. Even if only part of the system were privatized (just 5 percentage points) financial middlemen would be able to siphon off $150 billion of payroll taxes to increase their profits each year.

Although they don't want to be seen as spearheading the effort to privatize Social Security, companies such as American International Group Inc. (insurance), State Street Boston Corp. (pension company), American Express Corp., and Fidelity Investments are funding the public relations blitz in favor of privatization. These and likeminded companies, foundations, and individuals finance speeches and media campaigns that have so successfully highlighted the "crisis" in Social Security that, as former House Speaker Newt Gingrich (R-GA) was fond of saying, more people under the age of 30 believe in UFOs than believe that they will ever collect any money from Social Security. Privatization is then presented as the "fix" to a crisis that doesn't exist.

The push to privatize pensions in the United States is part of a global move to transfer public money to corporations and financial managers. In Chile, for example — a country that is often held up as a model by President Bush and others — the privatized pension system requires that 10 percent of workers' salaries be deposited in mutual funds and as much as a third of their contributions go to fees for the pension fund managers. Under the reformed Chilean system, at least half of all workers receive no pension from the government at all. The government minister of labor and social security, who oversees the program, told Larry Rother of the *New York Times* in January 2005, "It is absolutely impossible to think that a system of this nature is going to resolve the income needs of Chileans when they reach old age." Pension reform was initially forced on Chile during the rule of Augusto Pinochet when the World Bank threatened to deny badly needed loans unless the government made deep social security cuts.

Now the World Bank is pressing for pension reforms in many other countries in Latin America and elsewhere. Foreign firms, mainly from the United States, control a large segment of the global retirement fund management sector. Foreign private insurance companies are moving into the gigantic Chinese market as China sets up personal retirement funds for some workers and considers dismantling the social security system that had provided decent pensions for its retirees.

Women, particularly low-income women, have the most to lose from privatization. In the United States, women are 58 percent of the people on Social Security who are 62 years of age or older, and approximately 70 percent of those who are 85 and older. Relatively low-earning jobs, time away from the job market in order to raise families, and patterns of discrimination in the job market all contribute to women having low Social Security benefits in relation to men.

In spite of this, because most women receive no income from a pension, and because monthly benefits for retired women who do receive a pension average much less than those for retired men, Social Security is essential. In addition, Social Security provides disability benefits and survivors' benefits to families. Without this coverage, many more women would become destitute and would be unable to support dependents after an injury to, or the death of, their spouse. Finally, if basic benefits were reduced for the poor under privatization schemes, women could become the "silent shock absorbers" once again as they take on the care of aged parents with fewer means to be independent.

Medicare and Medicaid

Despite spending more money on healthcare than any other country, the United States is ranked very low compared to other countries on overall measures such as life expectancy and infant mortality, particularly for people of color. This is the only industrialized country that does not provide healthcare for all its citizens — 45 million people do not have health insurance. Yet that figure is misleading. A study done by Families USA in 2004 found that if you add in people who go without health insurance for part of a year, the number is 81.8 million people, one out of three people in the United States under age 65.

Over 85 percent of Medicaid recipients are women and children, and about 47 percent are African American. Low-income senior citizens spend a quarter of their income on medical care, while the richest fifth of the population spends 15 percent.

Medicare was created in 1965 as a federal health insurance program to make sure that the elderly would have adequate health coverage after they stopped working. It provides health insurance to 40 million people, about one out of every seven Americans. Medicare beneficiaries include 34 million people aged 65 and above, and about 5 million people below age 65 with physical disabilities. At age 61, women make up 57 percent of the recipients of Medicare, while at age 85 they make up 71 percent, since women, on average, live longer than men. Combined with Social Security, Medicare has made a substantive difference in the lives of elderly Americans and is particularly important for women.

Like Social Security, Medicare is an entitlement, meaning that all who qualify for the program must be covered. This means the budget has to accommodate whatever level of funding is needed each year. Also like Social Security, the Medicare system is run efficiently. Expenses for overhead and administration are less than 2 percent of the benefits paid out. In contrast, private insurance companies are estimated to have overhead rates of 12 to 14 percent or more, and the overhead in managed care organizations (i.e., Health Maintenance Organizations or HMOs) is often even higher.

The Bush administration and many conservatives want to privatize Medicare. The Medicare Prescription Drug Improvement and Modernization Act of 2003, which was passed by the Congress, is a step in that direction. According to the AFL-CIO, this bill does nothing to control drug prices and was written to benefit big drug companies, not people participating in Medicare. This legislation helps steer billions of dollars from taxpayers to the pharmaceutical industry.

Medicaid provides healthcare and long-term care services to more than 40 million low-income families, the elderly, and disabled people. It insures more than one in seven Americans and is the primary source of federal financial assistance to the states. Medicaid covers the cost of long-term care for conditions that Medicare does not cover, so it is essential for anyone with few assets or a chronic condition. Although Medicaid reaches many people, there are still millions of children who are eligible for Medicaid but who do not receive coverage because of poor outreach and other enrollment barriers.

In recent years, certain services previously provided through Medicaid have been privatized, particularly those in the area of mental health. This leads to the loss of public sector healthcare jobs, which, as we saw earlier, negatively affects women. In addition, more and more states are forcing Medicaid recipients into managed care, ostensibly to save money. This compromises their access to health-care and the quality of service they receive.

Fighting Privatization

These moves to privatization make it even more essential that women get involved in determining our national priorities so that safety nets are in place for everyone who needs them. George W. Bush has set an agenda for his second term that includes partial pri-vatization of Social Security combined with benefit cuts, tax reform to solidify the transfer of wealth upwards, cutbacks in government services, and increased military funding. Now is the time to clarify our alternative vision and to gather the courage to pursue it boldly.

Globally, national governments are finding their powers weak-ened and their public wealth depleted by trade policies that increase the power of corporations and consolidate international money flows in the hands of an elite group of money managers. This has a pro-found effect on women and people of color because they rely on gov-ernment support disproportionately, especially if they support children on their own or if they are elderly. According to the United Nations, women do two thirds of the world's work, but receive only 10 percent of the income. At the other end of the spectrum, in 2001, the world's 497 billionaires registered a combined wealth of $1.54 trillion, greater than the combined incomes of the poorest half of humanity.

Organizations and individuals across the United States and around the globe are working to strengthen their national governments and communities in the face of these trends. I offer *Women and the U.S. Budget* as a tool to bring women in the United States to the forefront of decisions about resource allocations and budget priorities.

PART 1

❖

Budget Basics

Yᴏᴜ ᴀʀᴇ ɴᴏᴡ ᴇɴᴛᴇʀɪɴɢ the land of the national budget. The money the government receives, holds, and spends belongs to all of us. In Part One — the next four chapters — we will explore where the money comes from, where the money goes, whether the budget is balanced or shows a surplus or deficit, and who decides.

As I suggested in the Preface, you might want to take on the role of a public investigator (PI) as you investigate the mysteries of the budget and how they affect women. I will give you "PI Pointers" as we go along to highlight some of the smokescreens and mirrors that hide budget realities.

CHAPTER 2

❖

Where Does the Money Come From?

THERE IS NOTHING MAGICAL about the income side of the budget, but the curiosity and persistence of a PI comes in handy when trying to understand it because much of the information available to the public is unclear. Little is known about how the Department of the Treasury prepares estimates of income for the government, and the budget documents themselves give scant information about income. The focus of the budget documents is on spending and government programs, downplaying the central role taxation plays in public policy.

Tax policy is important for the following reasons:

❖ It determines how much disposable income a family or household has.

❖ It determines which sectors of the population bear the biggest burden of supporting the government.

❖ It determines how much is available to the government for public programs.

Taxation has a huge impact on women as they participate in the labor force in greater numbers. The fastest-growing group of tax filers is "heads of households" — single, unmarried, or separated people supporting children on their own— and it is made up mostly of single mothers.

One thing to keep in mind as we look at taxation is that accounting is a key to understanding it. Accounting, which refers to the records the government keeps of its financial transactions, appears to be a neatly plowed field, but it is really a minefield. How the records are kept has consequences in the policy-making arena because it shapes how people think about the money. Another way of looking at it is to realize that *how* the records are kept is a political decision, reflecting certain assumptions and values. On the income side of the budget we will be walking through this minefield of accounting, especially when we look into certain tax laws. As we will see later on in the chapter, accounting methods play a large role in how public policy is implemented through the tax laws.

PI POINTER

When you think about accounting, remember the Enron scandal. One of the most successful companies in the world worked with one of the biggest accounting firms, Arthur Anderson, to use accounting tools that masked the truth. Accounting reflects values.

Think of the government's income as a great river of money made up of many streams. The source of each of these streams is the labor and productivity of workers and businesses, which create the wealth that is then available to be used by the government.

Congress passes tax laws in order to get the streams flowing. As the river of money comes in, it is used for various programs and services for which money has been appropriated.

It is important to keep in mind that the way the income streams are set up now is only one of several possible ways for configuring income, and decisions by Congress can change it at any time. Before we look at how things are set up now, though, let's take a look at some highlights on the path to the present system of taxation.

Background

From the time the first money-raising bill (a tax on imports) was passed in 1789, Congress has changed the income streams over and over again. The first income tax was enacted in 1862 to support the Civil War effort. The act of 1862 also created the Commissioner of Internal Revenue, the precursor to the Internal Revenue Service (IRS), which is now a division of the Department of the Treasury.

The Constitution explicitly forbade a national tax on income, but such a tax was legalized when the 16th Amendment was adopted in 1913. At that time Congress put in place an income tax that applied only to the richest 5 percent of households.

Between 1909 and 1941, most of the money the government received came from taxes on corporations. (Like taxes on individual income, corporate income taxes have gone through many changes over the years.) It was not until 1941 that individual income taxes became the main source of revenue for the government. The withholding tax on wages was introduced in 1943 and was key to increasing tax collections.

President Franklin D. Roosevelt signed the Social Security Act into law in 1935. It created another stream of individual income taxes: a payroll tax. The Social Security tax shows up on your pay stub as FICA, short for the Federal Insurance Contributions Act, which is phrasing from the original Social Security Act. The government began collecting Social Security taxes in 1937 and putting them in a trust fund — a fund the government could use to pay benefits, cover administrative costs, and invest in securities to earn interest. The programs associated with Social Security include Old-Age, Survivors, and Disability Insurance (OASDI), and Medicare.

From the beginning, the pressure to levy and increase individual income taxes has usually come from the government's need to raise money to fight wars or increase military spending. The great expansion in revenues necessary to enter into and sustain fighting in World War I, World War II, the Korean War, and the Vietnam War would not have been possible without Congress's power to tax income.

It has only been since World War II — particularly in the decades of the Cold War — that the IRS has developed its enormous bureaucracy of collection and enforcement. The writer Edmund Wilson, who was hounded by the IRS and had income seized for years, said that Americans were taught to fear two things — the Soviet Union and the IRS. As he pointed out, these two fears came together to insure income was raised to fund the large US military and weapons buildup during the Cold War.

Which brings us to an important point: Taxes are compulsory. If a person receives income but does not file a return with the IRS and does not pay any tax, he or she can be penalized if discovered by the IRS. Tax resisters face double fines (for both non-filing and non-payment). The IRS may start criminal prosecution, and it can seize wages, money in bank accounts, cars, homes, and other assets to pay tax bills. However, the more extreme actions and criminal penalties are unusual.

There is a long history of people who have refused to pay taxes for a variety of reasons across the political spectrum. Writer Henry David Thoreau became one of the most famous tax resisters when he spent a night in a Massachusetts jail for refusing to pay taxes to support the Mexican-American War of 1846. Tax resistance to wars reached a peak during the 1960s and 1970s, when more than 500,000 Americans openly opposed paying taxes to support the Vietnam War. Congressman Ronald Dellums (D-CA) introduced the World Peace Tax Fund Act in the 1970s to create a special "conscientious objector" status for taxpayers. Although the legislation has been introduced in every session of Congress since, it has yet to pass.

PI POINTER

You would have to spend over $5 million a day every day for one year in order to spend $1.8 trillion — what the government took in for fiscal year 2004 — in twelve months.

Sources of Federal Income

Now we will look at the major streams that currently make up the giant river of money. Figure 2.1 is drawn from the budget documents and summarizes the receipts (or income) side of the budget (to see

Receipts By Source — Summary

(In billions of dollars)

Source	2004 Actual	Estimate					
		2005	2006	2007	2008	2009	2010
Individual income taxes	809.0	893.7	966.9	1,071.2	1,167.2	1,245.1	1,353.3
Corporation income taxes.	189.4	226.5	220.3	229.8	243.4	252.4	257.6
Social insurance and retirement							
receipts.	733.4	773.7	818.8	866.2	911.7	959.1	1,016.2
(On-budget).	(198.7)	(212.4)	(225.6)	(237.0)	(247.2)	(258.4)	(273.0)
(Off-budget).	(534.7)	(561.4)	(593.2)	(629.2)	(664.6)	(700.7)	(743.2)
Excise taxes.	69.9	74.0	75.6	77.2	79.0	81.0	82.9
Estate and gift taxes	24.8	23.8	26.1	23.5	24.3	26.0	20.1
Customs duties.	21.1	24.7	28.3	30.6	31.9	33.9	35.3
Miscellaneous receipts	32.6	36.4	41.6	45.6	49.5	52.6	55.4
Total receipts.	1,880.1	2,052.8	2,177.6	2,344.2	2,507.0	2,650.0	2,820.9
(On-budget).	(1,345.3)	(1,491.5)	(1,584.4)	(1,715.0)	(1,842.4)	(1,949.3)	(2,077.7)
(Off-budget).	(534.7)	(561.4)	(593.2)	(629.2)	(664.6)	(700.7)	(743.2)

Source: Table S-8, Budget of the United States Government, Fiscal Year 2006.

figure 2.1

the budget documents, charts, and tables yourself, go to <www.gpoaccess.gov/usbudget/fy06/index.html/>).

Note that the numbers in Figure 2.1 are in billions of dollars, so the amount of individual income taxes in fiscal year 2004 was really $809,000,000,000 or $809 billion. The total receipts for 2004 were $1,880,100,000,000 or almost $1.8 trillion. This is what the river of money amounted to in 2004, and it is a lot of resources.

Figure 2.2 presents another way of looking at the same information.

As you will see, individual taxes are close to half the total sources of income. However, more than half of social insurance and retirement taxes also come from individuals, and some of the excise (or sales) taxes are on products that individuals consume, such as alcohol and cigarettes. This means that close to three quarters of the taxes the government collects come from individuals.

If you are employed, you are feeding into three of these streams: individual income taxes; social insurance and retirement (in the form of Social Security and Medicare, or FICA); and excise, or sales taxes. You are also paying state and in some cases local income taxes, sales taxes, and fees.

US Government Receipts by Source, Fiscal Year 2004

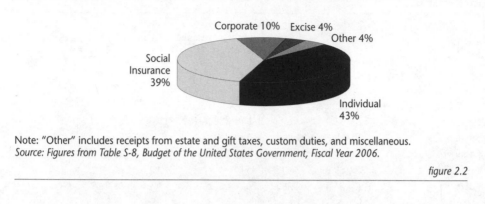

Note: "Other" includes receipts from estate and gift taxes, custom duties, and miscellaneous.
Source: Figures from Table S-8, Budget of the United States Government, Fiscal Year 2006.

figure 2.2

Now we will look at what the categories used in Figures 2.1 and 2.2 refer to.

Individual Income Taxes

Individual income taxes are based on your income. Individuals are taxed in a number of ways: on wages and salaries; tips; interest received; dividends; alimony received; business income; rental income; certain state and local tax refunds; certain pensions and annuities; private supplemental unemployment benefits; gambling income; capital gains; and some social security income.

If you are employed, you will fill out a W-4 form when you start your job. This tells the employer how much money to withhold from your paycheck to cover the federal, state, and, in some cases, local taxes you owe each year. The employer is required to take the money withheld from his or her employees' paychecks and deposit it in a Federal Reserve bank (see Chapter 6) or authorized financial institution each pay period or each month. This money streams into the Federal Reserve banks from every employer, and the government draws on these resources to pay for services and programs.

You are legally required to file a tax return every year. On the return you list all the money you made and all the taxes you paid. The information on how much you have paid is on the W-2 form, which your employer is required to give you in January of each year and which you send in with your taxes. Then you determine if you still owe any taxes or if you have paid too much and are eligible to receive a refund.

If you are self-employed, you pay income taxes directly to the government in four installments a year, based on what you paid the year before. This system is called estimated taxes.

Corporate Taxes

Corporations pay income taxes based on their profits. Some corporations pay no or few taxes due to tax breaks and lowered taxes on profits earned.

Twenty years ago, corporate taxes were a much bigger share of government income — more than twice what they are today — but tax laws were changed to reduce the amounts corporations owed. This means individual taxpayers now pay a larger share of the government's income, and corporate tax collections are at their lowest level in six decades. Many corporations also find ways to avoid paying taxes they do owe. Under tax changes made during the presidency of Ronald Reagan, corporations were allowed to write off purchases of machinery and equipment at a much faster rate than before.

According to the Government Accountability Office (GAO), 60 percent of US corporations failed to pay any tax from 1996 to 2000. In 2004, the Institute on Taxation and Economic Policy reported that 82 companies received rebate checks totaling $12.6 billion between 2001 and 2003. The largest tax breaks went to General Electric, SBC Communications, Citigroup, IBM, Microsoft, AT&T, and Exxon Mobil.

In 1986, the US Congress adopted the alternative minimum tax to reduce differences between what various companies paid and to insure every company that made a lot of profit was paying some tax. But legislation passed in 1993 and 1997 emasculated the tax. In 2002 and 2004 Congress passed more corporate tax breaks. Many corporations are once again paying less than zero in national income taxes.

Other Taxes

Employers are required to withhold and deposit Social Security and Retirement taxes (FICA) from their employees' paychecks. They must also make matching contributions. If you are self-employed, you pay the full amount of FICA yourself. These taxes are used to pay out benefits to current recipients of Social Security and Medicare programs. Social Security taxes currently generate a surplus each year (in other words, more is taken in than needs to be paid out to retirees

each year). The Social Security law requires that the surplus be loaned to the government — through the purchase of government bonds — and the government uses it to cover budgeted expenses.

Excise taxes are mostly sales taxes on specific items, including alcohol, tobacco, telephone service, gasoline, firearms, ammunition, and certain chemicals and other products. They also include user fees for highways and airports.

Estate taxes are paid on the money and property possessed by a person when he or she dies, while gift taxes are taxes paid by the giver when he or she gives another person property (including money) worth more than a set amount without expecting payment in return.

Custom duties are funds collected from taxes on imports and exports.

The Miscellaneous heading covers deposits of earnings by the Federal Reserve (the Federal Reserve banks are required to transfer a portion of their surplus after expenses to the US Treasury) and other miscellaneous receipts such as the sale of seized goods.

Tax Expenditures

Now we will investigate a mysterious part of the government's income known as tax expenditures. The "tax code" — the collection of laws enacted by the government that determines how income is collected — includes the income streams outlined above and tax expenditures. Tax expenditures are mysterious partly because they are completely invisible in the budget itself, yet they determine how a good portion of our national resources is used.

If you examine the official budget documents, you will see charts of income (like the ones in Figures 2.1 and 2.2) and expenses (which we will look at in Chapter 3) prominently displayed, but you will not see the tax expenditure programs. They are buried much farther back in the documents and are, in fact, in a different document altogether from the budget presentation. The government is required, by the Congressional Budget Act of 1974, to list these programs somewhere in the budget documents, but they are not accounted for in terms of money coming in and going out. In other words, this is where the accounting methods completely break down from the point of view of a PI. Because tax expenditures are not visible in the budget, one of the major ways the government distributes resources is hidden, and anyone who wants to understand this distribution will be confused.

Tax expenditure programs are administered through the tax code (and therefore are implemented by the IRS), in contrast to spending programs, which are implemented through the government agencies responsible for them. Tax expenditures range from the home mortgage interest deduction to subsidies for McDonald's to advertise abroad and reimbursements to defense contractors for mergers.

PI POINTER

"Tax expenditure" is the term used to describe a vast array of government programs designed to accomplish some social or economic goal by using the tax system.

If we go back to our image of streams of money to the government, tax expenditures are like negative streams, backwaters that have been created by dams at certain points. Some of them flow backwards and stay clear, and some are swamps. These streams never make it to the river, but if they did, the river would be much larger.

One way to understand tax expenditures is to think of them as a form of tax break, as money the government would normally collect but forgoes for a specific purpose. For instance, if the interest home-owners pay on their mortgages were taxed, it would bring in tens of billions of dollars each year. However, because of the home mortgage interest deduction, a tax expenditure program, this interest is not taxed. The government's loss of this revenue directly benefits one group of people — homeowners — but the resources are then not available to be spent on programs that would benefit other groups. For instance, people who prefer to rent or who cannot save for a downpayment get no support from the national tax system (although some states do help renters). As well, the government does not fully subsidize low-income housing, so someone who cannot afford market rents has a housing crisis.

The top tax expenditures are:

- ❖ taxes deferred or never paid on employer and employee contributions to retirement plans such as 401Ks and IRAs,
- ❖ taxes deferred on employer-paid health insurance for workers,
- ❖ the home mortgage interest deduction,
- ❖ capital gains, and
- ❖ a whole array of corporate tax breaks.

Some tax expenditures take the form of tax credits and tax exclusions. The government issues tax credits for certain expenditures and activities. Credits reduce the amount of taxes due, unlike a deduc-

PI POINTER

Over $100 billion a year goes to corporations, including those in such needy industries as insurance and oil and gas, through tax expenditures in the form of tax breaks.

tion, which reduces the amount of income to be taxed. (An example of a tax credit — the Earned Income Tax Credit (EITC) — is described below.) A tax exclusion is income or funding not subject to taxation, such as income received by charitable or religious organizations, or employer contributions for medical insurance premiums or medical care.

As PIs, we notice that programs benefiting upper-income earners and corporations often take the form of tax expenditures rather than direct payments from the expense budget. Since these programs are invisible in the budget — unlike most programs for poor and low-income people, which are shown in the expense side of the budget — they are less subject to public attention and scrutiny. In other words, an accounting trick hides the way the government helps to make the rich richer, while poor and low-income people are often accused of being too "dependent" on the government, an accusation that some groups use to justify cutting safety net programs.

One concern about tax expenditures is that many of the ones structured as personal deductions benefit those who have lots of resources more than poor people. And the richer a person is, the greater the benefit. For example, let's look at the home mortgage interest deduction again. You can deduct more interest if you are in a higher tax bracket. This is an upside-down benefit that would not likely remain as presently structured if it were a direct spending program. If it were visible in the budget, rather than being an invisible tax expenditure, people would question the fairness of such an arrangement.

Another example of a tax expenditure that benefits the wealthy disproportionately is the reduction in the capital gains tax. Taxes are due on capital gains after a person sells assets such as stocks, bonds, real estate, and artworks. However, there are limits on how much tax a person has to pay on capital gains, so the capital gains tax expenditure figure is money lost to the government.

Multinational corporations can take advantage of complex "transfer pricing" systems allowed by the tax code. The IRS determines how much of a company's worldwide earnings relate to its US activities and are therefore subject to US tax. As a result, companies try to shift *income* away from the United States and shift deductible expenses *into* the country. In the report "Hidden Tax Entitlements," Robert J. McIntyre used IBM as an example of how this works. In its annual report to stockholders in 1987, IBM said that a third of its worldwide profits were earned by its US operations. But on its federal tax return, IBM treated so much of its research and development expenses as US-related that it reported almost no US earnings. Despite $25 billion in US sales that year, the company owed no taxes.

McIntyre, director of Citizens for Tax Justice, points out that the cost of business and investment tax expenditures is now much more than the support for businesses in the form of spending programs. These business tax expenditures are only one part of a larger pattern of government support for corporations that we will be investigating.

PI POINTER

Welfare used to be an entitlement, meaning that anyone eligible who applied for it was supported, no matter what the cost to the government. Now welfare spending is limited, but entitlements for the middle class, wealthy and corporations are hidden in the tax code, a mountain of lost resources that keeps growing.

Another concern about tax expenditures is that they are not subject to as much cost review and evaluation as spending programs are. Tax expenditures are available to any individual or company that qualifies, and they tend to run on autopilot once they get into the tax code. In contrast, spending programs, such as those for environmental protection or for roads and community development, must be approved every year. Often, funding for these programs is limited by laws that set ceilings to control government spending. These programs often shrink as a percentage of government spending, while tax expenditures — which are not subject to any freeze or review — grow tremendously.

The invisibility of tax expenditures might be acceptable if these were relatively small programs. But tax expenditures (those that are business related as well as all the others, such as the home mortgage interest deduction) total close to $830 billion or the equivalent of a third of total budget expenses.

There are, however, tax expenditures that provide much-needed assistance and promote equity. The Earned Income Tax Credit (EITC) is one of the major tax credit programs. It was started in 1975 to off-set Social Security and Medicare taxes for low- and moderate-income working families. It is a refundable credit for individuals and families who earn less than a certain amount of income. The fact that it's

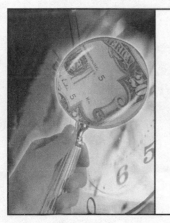

PI POINTER

Here's how the EITC benefits a single mom: Let's say she is raising two children and earned $10,000 in 2004. Her Social Security and Medicare payroll tax was $765. She Is eligible for an EIC of $4,000, which pays her back her payroll tax and gives her an EIC refund of $3,235.

refundable means that if the credit is more than what the family or individual owes in taxes, they will receive a check for the rest of the credit. The EITC moves more than 2 million children out of poverty, more than any other safety net program.

Another tax credit is the Child Tax Credit (CTC), for families with dependent children under age 17. It was worth up to $600 per child in 2002. The CTC has been in effect since 1998, and in 2001 Congress introduced changes that made the credit available to mil-lions more low- and moderate-income working families and gave many families a larger CTC than they would have received in the past. Like the EITC, the CTC is refundable, meaning some families can get the credit even if they owe no income tax.

Who Contributes?

The question of who contributes is a tricky one for PIs. As we have seen, tax laws create income streams from many sources and produce back eddies that drain off money, as in tax expenditures. When we want to understand the contributions of different sectors of society, we need to look at more than the total numbers. For instance, although wealthy individuals might pay a huge total amount of money in individual taxes, they could receive tax breaks that mean they pay a smaller percentage of their income than someone who makes less money.

PI POINTER

The government does not keep track of what percentage of taxes women pay, so we can't compare their contribution to what men pay.

The government decides not only how much money it wants to raise to cover government programs, but also *how* this money will be raised. For example, it knows it can raise money from individuals by passing income tax laws, but it still has to determine *how much* to raise from each individual, who will not have to pay taxes, and how it will collect the taxes owed. Our next step in uncovering clues about where the government's income comes from is to look at how the taxes are structured.

Tax Rates

As mentioned earlier, the tax code is the collection of laws that guide the way taxes are assessed and collected. It covers such details as the rates at which people and corporations must pay taxes, as well as when and how the taxes must be paid. The US tax code is huge and complex, containing 7 million words and almost 6,000 pages (you can view it online at <www.fourmilab.ch/ustax/ustax.html>). Its complexity makes the income side of the budget a mystery for regular people. It also gives people who have the resources to hire tax lawyers and tax accountants an advantage at tax payment time.

The part of the tax code that sets out what individual taxpayers pay is progressive. This means that the rate at which income is taxed rises as income rises, so people with higher incomes pay more of their income to the government. This is designed to make the system fair, as people with a higher income will theoretically pay a higher proportion of the costs of government programs that benefit everyone. However, wealthy people eligible for various tax credits and exemptions often have access to lawyers who help them figure out how to pay as little tax as possible. And,because of lax enforcement on the part of the IRS, people with high incomes often pay a smaller proportion of their income in taxes than those with low and moderate incomes.

PI POINTER

Between 2002 and 2012, the richest taxpayers — those with incomes in the top one percent — in the United States will receive, on average, $342,000 each in tax cuts, while most taxpayers will receive, on average, $350 each.

Individual tax rates start at 15 percent and go up to 35 percent (as of 2005), with the exact rate determined by your marital status (i.e., whether you are single, married, or the head of a household). It is important to remember that the tax is figured on taxable income, not gross income. The tax rate therefore applies to income after various deductions and exemptions have been taken.

Income tax changes that favor those with the most income and assets, such as the tax breaks enacted by the George W. Bush administration and Congress in 2003, contribute to the massive increases in wage and income inequality that have occurred in the United States over the past 20 years. In 1997, the richest one percent of households had 40 percent of the nation's household wealth. They had more wealth than the entire bottom 95 percent.

Other taxes on income include payroll contributions to Social Security and Medicare (FICA). This tax is paid equally by employer and employee on every dollar of wages and salary up to $90,000 (as of 2005) of income. After that there is no tax. The Medicare part of FICA is paid on every dollar with no ceiling. If you are self-employed, you pay the combined amount.

Capital gains taxes are collected after a person sells his or her capital assets such as stocks, bonds, real estate, and artworks. Since taxes are collected only after an asset is sold, investors don't have to pay any taxes as long as they hold onto their assets. When they do sell, they can reduce these taxes by reporting capital losses at the same time, which are deducted from what is due.

Some income is not taxable, including child support payments and Temporary Assistance for Needy Families (TANF); life insurance proceeds received after a death; money received for an accident or health insurance claim; property received as a gift or inheritance; benefits administered by the Department of Veteran's Affairs; and money received under the Worker's Compensation Act for occupational sickness and injury. Also, some or all of the benefits received under Social Security or equivalent Railroad Retirement Benefits may not be taxed if they are your only income.

Not everyone is required to pay national taxes. It makes sense that people who earn very little are allowed to keep this money to cover basic expenses. Two decades ago the federal government acknowledged that taxing poor families was counterproductive and unfair. As part of the Tax Reform Act of 1986, virtually all families below the poverty line were excused from the requirement to pay federal income tax. By 1997, half of the states had implemented the same policy.

As PIs, we need to consider the whole tax situation people face. Federal taxes are not the only taxes people pay. They also pay state and local taxes. State taxes tend to be more regressive, which means everyone pays the same amount, regardless of income. Low- and moderate-income people pay the same as the very wealthy. This is "regressive" because the tax takes a proportionally bigger bite out of the income of people near the bottom and in the middle. Wealthy people may pay more money in total, but it's a lower portion of their income. Poor people or the working poor pay the highest portion of their incomes on these taxes, thereby bearing more of the burden of taxation in those instances. In the early 1990s, many states lowered personal income taxes — a boon to the rich — and increased sales taxes, which are another form of regressive tax. This meant that the rich had more disposable income and the poor, or people with moderate incomes, had less.

As is the case with the federal government, there is often a lack of information from the state governments about the impact of state tax policy on different sectors of the population.

Underlying Contributions: The Care Economy and Earth

As PIs look into the issue of who contributes the money that makes up the income streams to the government, they begin to understand that important contributions can be overlooked or discounted. It is our job to shine the light on these hidden contributions and to understand some of the more visible ones. When we think of the river of money streaming into the government, it is important to remember that this river could not flow without the wealth produced by workers. Workers work, earn salaries in exchange for that work, and then the government takes part of that income to pay for public programs. The workers' labor also helps to generate a surplus — profit — for their employers, who are then also taxed by the government.

However, none of this wealth from workers would be available to be taxed and used by the government without the activity of the care economy, which is invisible in official economic measurements. The care economy includes all the wealth-producing and life-sustaining activities, institutions, and relationships not counted in the official economy.

Much of this care economy consists of the goods and services provided within and by all the households in the United States. This includes meal preparation, sewing, laundry, child and elder care, home repairs, volunteering, produce from gardens, and transportation services using private automobiles. Women provide most of the goods and services in this invisible economy, but their contribution is not counted, valued, or compensated for in our economic or budget measures. The US budget exists in the context of this unacknowledged contribution, which is worth hundreds of billions of dollars a year to the country. This is the deeper foundation of the US budget and the economy, since the care economy provides services for free that would otherwise have to be provided or subsidized by government or other sectors of the economy.

At an even deeper level, Earth and its ecosystems provide an underlying contribution. Without the resources of Earth, nothing could be produced, and no wealth could be generated for households, corporations, or the government. Because standard economics — which is based on money — leaves out the contribution of Earth and the cost of economic development on the environment, it skews what we recognize as having worth and what we value. (These issues are discussed further in Chapter 6.)

Who Benefits?

Who benefits from the way the US tax structure is currently set up? There are many ways to answer this question. Everyone in the country benefits from the services and programs that the government funds with our tax dollars. These services and programs — which include the physical infrastructure of the country, grants to states and local communities for a variety of programs, education, housing, healthcare subsidies, and programs like the national parks, environmental protection, Medicare and Social Security — enable communities and individuals to function. Low-income people benefit from the EITC, as well as from Medicaid (the government health program for the poor), income and housing subsidies, and programs like Head Start. However, these programs are not fully funded, which means they do not serve all people who need the program.

When we ask who benefits, we need to look at overall fairness and lack of fairness in the tax structure. As we have seen, businesses and corporations benefit disproportionately from the tax structure in many ways, including through tax expenditures. Wealthy individuals benefit from the tax system through tax breaks, lower tax rates, and a lower overall tax bill if you take into account the total amount of taxes they pay, including state and local taxes. The middle class benefits from the tax system through such things as the home mortgage interest deduction.

Taxation has a huge impact on women who are struggling to find their place in the economy. As mentioned earlier, the fastest-growing group of tax filers is single people supporting children. Most of them have incomes that are not growing. In fact, single mothers today are worse off than the single mothers of 1970, and nearly twice as many adult women as men live below the poverty line. This has a dispro-portionate impact on people of color. A large number of families in those communities are maintained by women alone: close to half the families in the African-American community, and a quarter of the fam-ilies in the Latino community.

Tax policy is a central issue for women because it is one of the main factors influencing the flow of resources into their lives. One example is the Earned Income Tax Credit, discussed above, which can make the difference between a family being able to meet basic necessities or not. This is particularly important for women who are leaving welfare for jobs that do not pay enough to lift them out of poverty. Welfare recipients who take jobs have average earnings of $8,000 to $10,800 per year, which is not enough to raise a family of three or four above the poverty level.

However, although the EITC provides financial relief for the work-ing poor, when a household begins to earn more in the workforce, the EITC is phased out, which increases the tax burden on low-income families. This is because the government takes away the EITC bene-fit, which has become a key part of the resources of the family, and at the same time it begins to tax the worker at regular rates. For many workers in the low-income bracket, this means they are shoulder-ing the same high level of taxation as solidly middle-class taxpayers.

Married working mothers also often find that their contribution to the family's economic picture is compromised by the outdated tax structure. When they file as part of a couple, their joint earnings push them into a higher tax bracket than they would be in on their own, even if they only earn the minimum wage. As a result they lose a lot of the buying power of their earnings, while also having to pay exor-bitant costs for childcare to make their employment possible. Some changes were made to this situation in 2003 — for instance, the stan-dard deduction for couples was doubled — but they are temporary changes and do not comprehensively deal with the challenges many working women find in trying to balance work and family.

I described the Child Tax Credit earlier, but it is only worth hun-dreds of dollars, barely enough to cover a few months of childcare for one child. Although the Child Care and Development Block Grant offers a subsidy for childcare, only one in seven families who need it receives the subsidy.

PI POINTER

Businesses can take a direct tax deduction for meals and entertainment, but a working-class mother cannot deduct her childcare expenses.

Obviously, higher wages, pay equity, and decent benefits are just as important to women's economic lives as tax policy, but taxes are a key part of the puzzle that need more attention.

Low-income, working-class, and middle-class women have been particularly hard hit by increases in the Social Security payroll tax and the state and local taxes (like sales taxes) that take a bigger bite out of the incomes of low-income families. In fact, Donald L. Barlett and James B. Steele, award-winning investigative journalists, revealed how Social Security and Medicare taxes (taken out of paychecks as FICA) are actually double taxes — or as they refer to it, "a tax upon a tax" — that hit working Americans hard. In a 2003 article in *Time* magazine, they show how a family earning $60,000 in wage income has $3,720 deducted for Social Security taxes and $870 for Medicare. The family never sees that $4,590, but it is considered to be part of their taxable personal income, and it is taxed as if the family received it.

In contrast, when President George W. Bush proposed the elimination of double taxation on stock dividends, he said: "It is unfair to tax money twice." However, eliminating the tax on dividends primarily benefits the very wealthy. Charles Schwab, founder of the discount brokerage firm and one of the main advocates for ending the tax on dividends, would save $4 million on his tax bill if this proposal became law.

In the past 20 years, tax policy has been a major instrument for an upward distribution of wealth, which has benefited the very wealthy and corporations. Hidden entitlements for the wealthy and corporations reduced income to the government by hundreds of billions of dollars a year at the same time that public services and social programs were being cut. In the next chapter we'll look at how the government decides which of those services and programs to fund and how much money to spend on each of them.

CHAPTER 3

❖

Where Does the Money Go?

NOW THAT WE HAVE INVESTIGATED THE INCOME SIDE of the budget, it is time to turn to the expense side of the budget. This is where the rivers of public resources that stream in through the tax system flow out to various programs and sectors of society. In this chapter, we will look for answers to the questions:

❖ Where does the money go?

❖ Who benefits?

The more closely we look at the expenses, the clearer it becomes that, just as all women's lives are connected to what happens in Washington, so are all sectors of society interdependent with the government. All of us receive a part of that flow of money and resources. One person may use the income support programs, another may rely on Social Security, and a third benefits from special education programs funded by the government, while everyone uses the roads, and corporations get subsidies. We are all dependent, all part of the flow. In fact, payments and special programs for corporations cost far more in the national spending plan than programs like welfare, which benefit poor and low-income women.

One reason the expense side of the budget is so crucial for women and people of color is that they are discriminated against in the economy, despite some economic gains in recent decades. Women and people of color experience higher unemployment, are concentrated in lower-paying jobs, and have less wealth (assets, property, stocks, bonds, savings, pensions, etc.) than men. Most women work in the service sector in jobs that pay little money, provide few or no benefits, and demand part-time and/or irregular hours. All of this means women need to rely on certain government services and programs more than men in order to insure a decent quality of life for themselves and the children or elders they support. Yet in the last 20 years, many of the programs women rely on for income support have been singled out by Congress to be cut back, including welfare, Medicaid, low-income housing programs, Medicare, student loans, food stamps, and Supplemental Security Income for disabled children and immigrants.

Diane Dujon, a former welfare recipient who is now a professor and organizer at the University of Massachusetts, has observed that "government is the only trust fund for people who live half a world away from Wall Street."[1] Until women are able to thrive within the economy, with or without a male partner, the government will continue to be a trust fund for them.

Government spending decisions also have an impact on women because women tend to be the "silent shock absorbers" when government spending is cut back. Since women provide most of the uncompensated and unrecognized childcare, supervision of young people, home maintenance, community volunteering, and elder care, they will do most of the extra work if national spending to address these needs is reduced. This means that how the resources are divided on the expense side of the budget affects the use of women's energy and can increase or decrease the stress in women's lives. If the full extent of women's contributions were calculated and taken into account, it would be obvious that women contribute vastly more to the nation than they receive from government programs.

Women are currently being deeply affected by the budget priorities of the Bush administration. Programs such as Medicaid, Supplemental Security Income, food stamps, Temporary Assistance for Needy Families, childcare, and the State Children's Health Insurance Program — all programs primarily used by women and their children — are slated for large cuts. Huge tax cuts, which primarily benefit the rich, and large military spending increases have been used as excuses for cutting these key social programs.

Background

Although spending the public's money is the primary activity of Congress, and therefore the core manifestation of our democracy, most members of Congress don't really have a full grasp of the budget. Outside of a few members on the budget committees, some congressional staffpeople, certain corporate and organizational lobbyists, academics who teach and study Congress, and those advocates for certain issues who study the budget closely, no one understands the whole picture of how, where, and on what the government spends the public's money. Even many of the people listed above understand only the small part of the budget that is their specialty.

According to Stanley Collender, author of the *Guide to the Federal Budget,* the Budget Enforcement Act of 1990 (BEA), one of the most significant changes ever made in the budget process, was conceived in such a way that "probably no more than half a dozen members of Congress, congressional staff, and Bush administration officials really knew and understood the implications of what was being discussed." It was passed in a rush, in virtual secrecy, and with no public hearings.

PIs need to be concerned about this in the context of national spending because the BEA put severe constraints on nonmilitary spending. This made it difficult to increase funding to much-needed programs that benefited many women, and in some cases it forced further cuts in those programs.

The veil of secrecy that surrounded the BEA illustrates how some entities (such as corporations and the military) and some classes (families with large incomes and/or huge wealth) who can afford to lobby government and have access to the budget creation process exercise a disproportionate influence on the use of public resources. This lack of democracy extends beyond Congress's handling of our annual national expenses. We, the public, are also owners of vast assets that the government holds, such as public lands (one third of the country), the public airwaves, and government property, yet we currently have little influence in how they are used or maintained or whether they are leased or sold.

Keep in mind that government spending is a flexible economic tool as well as a way to support programs each year, although the best way to use this tool is hotly debated in government and financial circles. Government spending can be used to keep the economy stable during a downturn in the economy (a recession), when businesses and individuals tend to curtail their spending, tax receipts go down, and more social services are needed. It can also be used to lessen class inequality through income support programs, tax policy, and unemployment insurance that helps workers during times of crisis in the economy. In the last 20 years, many of these programs have been cut and tax policies have been revised to benefit the wealthy and corporations at the expense of people at the bottom of the economic ladder.

Each year, spending decisions are determined in a political climate that can change due to many factors including the political relationship of the president and Congress, the power of corporations, the state of the economy, the needs of various interest groups, the effectiveness of organizing for social change, and the influence of big money in congressional elections and decisions.

As we did in the previous chapter on tax policy, we will look at how things are currently set up on the expense side of the budget, but keep in mind that federal spending reflects the values and assumptions of the people who put the budget together. The budgeting process is about making political choices and arranging the numbers and flows to satisfy those political choices; it is not necessarily about economic or social rationality. This means that it can be reconstructed and redesigned according to different values and realities. It also means that spending is presented in an accounting framework that serves the values of the people making the decisions, just as taxation is.

One example of how the framework can be adjusted is the use of off-budget programs. Currently only the huge Social Security trust fund and the US Postal Service are off-budget. These are programs that are kept out of the yearly budget limits or laws. However, Congress and the president use "off-budget" as a tool when they need it. In the past, programs ranging from the savings-and-loan bailout to the strategic petroleum reserve have been off-budget. Off-budget programs are counted with the on-budget programs to form what is known as the unified budget. The deficit is calculated from the unified budget, so any surplus from the Social Security budget helps to make the deficit smaller than it would otherwise be.

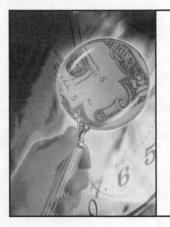

PI POINTER

Another slippery accounting issue: Social Security is sometimes on-budget and sometimes off-budget. This is because the Social Security money sits in a large trust fund and can affect how big the deficit looks. It was first put on-budget to mask the costs of the Vietnam War.

Spending

Each year Congress and the president must agree on a budget for the fiscal year (October through September) that determines what resources will be allocated to the various functions of government. Congress has a lot of resources to deal with, given that the budget is now well over $2 trillion a year. Even so, sometimes the government has more expenses than income in a given year, which means the budget is in a deficit situation. When the government has more income than expenses, it means there is a surplus.

In Chapter 2 you learned about the streams of money into the government. These are collected at Federal Reserve banks and other financial institutions and transferred to the Department of the Treasury. They are then paid out to various government agencies and programs according to the allocations in the budget.

In some ways, the federal expense part of the national budget is like your household budget. Your budget is divided into categories based on what you need and want to purchase to meet your family's (or your own) needs. Your budget (or your spending plan if you don't keep a formal budget) is divided into the following categories:

❖ Mandatory things (necessities) like water, food, rent or mortgage payments, clothing, fuel for heating and cooking, car or other transportation, childcare, taxes, loan repayments.

❖ Discretionary things like entertainment and eating out, vacations, hobbies, and charitable contributions.

❖ Long-term investments like a retirement plan (if it is not fully covered by your employer or if you are self-employed); a college fund for yourself or your children; or savings for a mortgage, home improvements, or other future goals.

How much you allocate to these different categories says a lot about what you think is important and how you balance present needs and wants with future goals. You will also make calculations about whether it makes sense to go into debt to meet current expenses in order to reach your long-term goals. If you don't have enough to cover monthly expenses (perhaps because you are unemployed, underemployed, the sole support of children and on welfare, in a low-wage job, elderly, or disabled), you either go into debt to meet necessities or you and your family do without – or both. Whatever your level of resources, though, you and your family are constantly making decisions about what is most important. Whether you have a formal budget or not, these monthly and daily decisions are part of how you care for yourself and your family. The national budget is a reflection of how we are caring for each other in this country.

Women, especially women supporting children on their own, often find themselves in the situation of not having enough to cover monthly needs, let alone generate a surplus that could pay for further education, retirement, or buying a house. Elderly women often have to choose between medicine and food or heating fuel or a visit to the grandchildren. As PIs we know that these personal decisions are connected to decisions made in Washington about what is important and what is not important.

In the same way that your personal budget plan reveals what is important to, or necessary for, you, the expense side of the US budget reveals the values and priorities of the United States government. Remember that your spending budget is divided into mandatory (the things you must pay) and discretionary (you choose how to handle these items). That's also how the government divides up the national spending side of the budget. Figure 3.1 shows the national expense side of the budget.

The chart in Figure 3.1 is from the US budget documents and shows discretionary and mandatory spending . Outlay is the budget term for dollars spent or expected to be spent on a certain activity —

in other words, spending. (As a PI, you can begin to familiarize your-self with the documents themselves at <www.gpoaccess.gov/ usbud-get/fy06/index.html>.)

Budget Summary by Category
(In billions of dollars)

	2004	2005	2006	2007	2008	2009	2010
Outlays:							
Discretionary:							
DOD military............	436	443	424	426	445	466	483
Non-DOD..............	459	487	497	491	488	486	488
Total, Discretionary	895	930	922	917	932	952	971
Proposed Supplemental......	–	35	25	18	2	1	–
Mandatory:							
Social Security...........	492	515	540	567	596	630	665
Medicare...............	181	194	199	209	225	245	266
Medicaid and SCHIP.......	181	194	199	209	225	245	266
Other	299	337	331	319	324	328	351
Total, Mandatory	1,237	1,337	1,410	1,476	1,551	1,635	1,743
Net Interest.............	160	178	211	245	272	294	314
Total Outlays...............	2,292	2,479	2,568	2,656	2,758	2,883	3,028
Receipts	1,880	2,053	2,178	2,344	2,507	2,650	2,821
Deficit.................	-412	-427	-390	-312	-251	-233	-207
On-budget deficit...........	-567	-589	-560	-506	-466	-463	-460
Off-budget surplus	155	162	170	194	215	230	252

Source: Table S-10, Budget of the United States Government, Fiscal Year 2006.

figure 3.1

You will notice that discretionary spending is broken down into "DOD (for Department of Defense) military" and "Non-DOD." "Defense" is the official budget term, but I call it "Military" in Figure 3.3 because I believe that is a more accurate term than defense (most of the spending in this category has nothing to do with defense), and as PIs we should be giving things their correct names. Note that by putting "DOD military" first and lumping all other discretionary spending together as "Non-DOD," the government defines those other programs in relation to military spending, indicating the promi-nent position of the military part of the budget and implying the rest of the programs are "leftovers" or somehow less important.

Figure 3.2 shows another way to look at this information for Fiscal Year 2004.

US Government Spending, Fiscal Year 2004

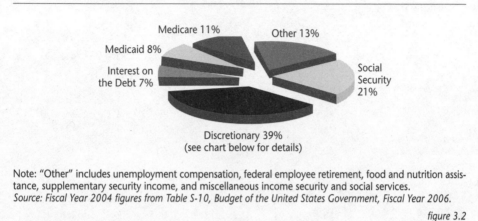

Discretionary 39%
(see chart below for details)

Note: "Other" includes unemployment compensation, federal employee retirement, food and nutrition assistance, supplementary security income, and miscellaneous income security and social services.
Source: Fiscal Year 2004 figures from Table S-10, Budget of the United States Government, Fiscal Year 2006.

figure 3.2

As Figure 3.2 shows, a large portion of national resources go to programs in the mandatory category like Social Security, Medicare, and interest on the federal debt. The rest of the budget is known as discretionary spending and includes housing, education, military spending, jobs and training programs, roads, bridges, mass transit, government administration, international aid, industry subsidies, community and regional development, aid to the states and federal government, environmental programs, science, technology, and community health programs. These discretionary expenses are broken down in Figure 3.3 below.

This figure shows that the military receives over half of discretionary spending. Therefore, after mandatory spending and the military portion of discretionary spending are taken out of the expense side of the budget, only a small percentage of national resources is left for everything else. Levels of funding for each discretionary program — including the military — are decided each year in the annual budget process. (See Chapter 5 for more on the process.)

The tables and graphs I've included give a broad overview of the expense side of the budget, but the budget documents get very specific about how much is allocated for each program. The president's budget proposal each year breaks the budget into what are called

US Government Discretionary Spending

	0	10	20	30	40	50	60	70	80	90	100

Military

Education, Employment,
Training, Social Services

Energy, Environment,
Science, Agriculture

Housing,
Income Security

Community & Regional
Develop., Transportation

Government
Administration

Health

International Affairs

Administration of Justice

Veterans' Affairs

Source: Fiscal Year 2004 from Table 8.7, Historical Tables, Budget of the United States Government, Fiscal Year 2006.

figure 3.3

"functions" (see Figure 3.4), which group spending according to its purpose (i.e., whether it's going to the military, agriculture, science and technology, etc). Within those functions are "line items" for each

PI POINTER

The national budget, like all of life, is filled with trade-offs. Here is one example from one state: Taxpayers in California are paying $752 million a year for ballistic missile defense (the most expensive single item in the military budget). For this same amount of money, California could fund 92,971 Head Start places for children.

US Budget Functions

Function number	Budget function
050	National defense
150	International affairs
250	General science, space, and technology
270	Energy
300	Natural resources and environment
350	Agriculture
370	Commerce and housing credit
400	Transportation
450	Community and regional development
500	Education, training, employment, and social services
550	Health
570	Medicare
600	Income security
650	Social Security
700	Veterans benefits and services
750	Administration of justice
800	General government
900	Net interest
920	Allowances
950	Undistributed offsetting receipts

figure 3.4

specific program. (We will see in Chapter 5 that these are related to the appropriations bills that must be passed each year.)

So, for example, Function 500 is "Education, employment, training and social services," under which fall many line items for programs such as the Child Care and Development Block Grant — a program that helps working parents hold down jobs, pay taxes, and stay off government support by subsidizing childcare. Each of the hundreds of programs on the expense side of the budget is an individual line item and must be approved in the course of the annual budget process.

Budget Rules and Expenses

If you want to get a deeper understanding of the expense side of the budget, it helps to look at the very particular definitions "mandatory" and "discretionary" have in the national budget. Mandatory spending is spending for which Congress has defined special eligibility and payment rules that apply over the long term. Everyone who meets those requirements and is enrolled in the program will receive payments. The amount paid out for the program will change depending on how many people need the program in any given year. By law the government is required to pay out that amount, no matter what it is. This is called an entitlement. Most mandatory programs are entitlements.

An example is the food stamps program. All the people who are eligible and registered to receive food stamps receive them, and the government foots the bill each year. During a downturn in the economy more people need food stamps, so the program will cost more than it does in a year when the economy is stronger. Some people may be eligible for food stamps but do not receive them, usually because they don't realize they are eligible, don't know how to sign up, or face other barriers to participation. This is one of the reasons many national and local organizations do benefits outreach work in communities so that eligible people can receive the income and tax breaks for which they qualify.

In contrast to mandatory spending, discretionary spending is determined by Congress each year. The people preparing the budget look at the pool of resources available for discretionary spending, they look at the discretionary programs, and they decide how to allocate the money through appropriations. An appropriation gives federal agencies the legal authority to make payments from the Treasury for specified purposes in a given year. (For example, the Department of Housing and Urban Development oversees such programs as homeless assistance and low-income housing assistance, or the Department of Health and Human Services oversees such programs as Head Start and Temporary Assistance for Needy Families.) In other words, an appropriation commits a certain amount of money for each program to be spent that year. This leaves nonmilitary discretionary programs (remember that the military currently takes up half of discretionary spending) vulnerable to being scaled back when members of Congress are searching for ways to cut spending in the budget.

Who Benefits?

Now that you have a general idea how the expense side of the budget is set up, we'll take a look at who benefits from the way expenses are handled. One example of how nonmilitary discretionary spending has been affected in recent years is provided by the Community Development Block Grant (CDBG). CDBG is a line item under the Department of Housing and Urban Development. For 25 years it has provided essential support to low- and moderate-income neighborhoods in over 1,000 communities. It has helped to build houses, playgrounds, and businesses and supports local decision making by allowing communities to decide how they want to spend the money. Two of the critical needs in low- and moderate-income neighborhoods are housing and jobs, and between 1994 and 1996, CDBG dollars were used to build or rehabilitate 641,000 affordable housing units and to create 445,000 new jobs.

PI Pointer

Women are the majority of the recipients of Social Security, Medicare, Medicaid, and social programs such as housing subsidies. This increases as they age — after age 85, they are 70 percent of those who receive Social Security and 71 percent of those who receive Medicaid and Medicare.

However, Congress has cut CDBG funding by over 41 percent since 1980, even though the needs in low- and moderate-income neighborhoods have increased during that period. At the same time, military spending was protected from deep cuts and then began rising again. Because the Budget Enforcement Act put a limit on how high discretionary spending could go, the increases in military spending have actually been financed by cuts in programs like CDBG. In this case, the beneficiaries are the military-related industries and contractors. As Congress prepares the 2006 budget, President Bush has proposed eliminating CDBG funding altogether.

Although most of the federal budget goes to mandatory programs (such as Social Security, Medicare, and Medicaid), only a third of the benefits of these programs go to poor and low-income people. When you combine this with the small percentage of discretionary spending that goes to programs benefiting people with low and moderate incomes, you can see that poor and low-income people are not the primary beneficiaries of national resource distribution, despite the rhetoric that support of poor and low-income people is busting the budget. This rhetoric was used to justify eliminating welfare as an entitlement, making it a block grant, and putting limits on how long women could receive it. This was done without providing adequate supports in the form of childcare, transportation, job training, and health coverage that are needed to insure a viable transition to the working world.

Even though programs benefiting poor and low-income people are a relatively small percentage of the budget and do not reach everyone who is eligible, they have proven to be very beneficial. According to Census Bureau data (as reported by the Center on Budget and Policy Priorities), federal antipoverty programs have lifted millions of children and disabled and elderly people out of poverty. Many of those who remained poor were significantly less poor than they would have been without government assistance.

Another issue to consider is the fact that the benefit levels of many government programs poor and low-income people rely upon are determined according to an official poverty line that vastly understates the real extent of poverty. Non-government researchers estimate that a family of four needs an income much higher than the official poverty line of $19,350 (as of 2005)to buy sufficient food, housing, healthcare, transportation, clothing, and other personal and household items, as well as pay taxes. This does not include many things, such as paid childcare, and it doesn't provide for people who can't find low-cost housing. Under this reconfigured poverty line, one in four people in the United States lives below the poverty line; 51 percent of African American women live below it, as do 66.9 percent of African American children under the age of six.

Military Spending
When we are investigating who benefits, it is important to look at two parts of the spending budget, one visible and one invisible — at least to the untrained eye. The visible portion is military spending,

and the invisible portion is corporate welfare. They are usually thought of as separate, but the vast majority of military spending is really part of corporate welfare. Many people don't think of military spending as corporate welfare because it has been so central a part of our national spending for so many decades. However, the major beneficiaries of military spending are corporations (called "defense contractors" in government lingo) that make huge profits from their contracts with the government, much higher than they could make on their own in the private market.

The actual costs of the military are in many ways obscured from us, even though it is obvious that it has a prominent place in the national spending plan. For five decades our government has subsidized the military industry to the tune of $19 trillion in public expenditures. This investment has produced the most advanced military technology in the world, supported industries that stock the military arsenal — aerospace, communications, and electronics — and created a lot of jobs. These jobs, however, went mostly to white males, and the same amount of money invested in civilian goods and services

SELF-SUFFICIENCY

A family of three earning $15,260 per year is living on the threshold of poverty, but does not meet the technical definition of "poor." In Metro West [outside of Boston] however, $15,260 is a third of what a family of three needs to meet basic needs, according to the Women's Educational and Industrial Union's 1999 study. A family of three consisting of one adult and two school-age children needed $45,357 per year in order to make ends meet. The Women's Union, in partnership with the Massachusetts Family Economic Self-Sufficiency Project, took a realistic look at the income needed to survive in the state and compiled its Self-Sufficiency Standard.

The standard takes into account a 28 percent increase in the cost of living in the Boston area over the last five years, led by a 61 percent increase in housing and child care costs. Housing is not the only important issue confronting low- to moderate-income residents in Massachusetts.

The Self-Sufficiency Standard sets this realistic monthly budget for a family of three:
- Housing, $1,343
- Child care, $688
- Food, $445

would have provided millions more jobs than can be provided through the military, many of them in fields such as teaching and public service where most employees are women.

The average American family has spent well over $50,000 in taxes on the military over 30 years. This level of military spending has been maintained even though we spend many times the amount that all our possible combat enemies, combined, pay for their military requirements, and even though we have already spent tens of billions on unnecessary and dangerous weapons. Even since September 11, 2001, and the war in Iraq, more of our military spending goes toward Cold War-era weapons than goes to the war on terrorism. Several of these weapons are deemed unnecessary and wasteful by military experts and are plagued by huge cost overruns that enrich military contractors and drain our public resources.

For a decade after the Cold War the US military budget was reduced by relatively small amounts each year, with workers and communities, and especially people of color, absorbing the brunt of those reductions. Between 1990 and 2000, hundreds of thousands of defense-related

- Transportation, $227
- Health care, $225
- Miscellaneous (clothing and household supplies) $293
- Taxes, $738

"We see this as a concrete measurable way to ensure the long-term economic viability of the region," said Mary M. Lassen, president and CEO of the Women's Union. It is particularly important in this era of welfare reform. According to the study: "As many parents leave welfare and enter the labor market, they join a growing number of families who are unable to stretch their wages to meet the costs of basic necessities."

The Women's Union isn't looking for entitlement programs, Lassen said. Instead, it suggests the state and federal government make investments in education and training "so that more Massachusetts residents can work toward the all-important goal of economic security."

From an editorial in *Metro West Daily News*, May 3, 2003. For more on the Self-Sufficiency Standard, see the Women's Educational and Industrial Union website <www.weiu.org>.

jobs disappeared. Profits for the defense industries, however, continued to outperform the stock of nondefense companies, and in 2002, President Bush initiated a budget process that included large increases in military spending, bringing the United States back to spending levels not seen since the peak of the Cold War. Of the $458-billion military budget for fiscal year 2004, only $28 billion went to homeland security and the war on terrorism.

Corporate Welfare

So who really benefits from these high levels of military spending? This is in some ways the ultimate corporate welfare. Defense contractors get massive subsidies from tax money. Military aid and the threat of intervention in developing countries are used to maintain a friendly climate for corporate exploitation abroad. Corporations also make arms and sell them to developing countries, which increases the chance of violence and civil war. Then we are told we have to protect ourselves against these violent countries. One example of this was spelled out in a *Washington Post* article by Michael Dobbs in 2002: "The administrations of Ronald Reagan and George H.W. Bush authorized the sale to Iraq of numerous items that had both military and civilian applications, including poisonous chemicals and deadly biological viruses, such as anthrax and bubonic plague." In 2003, the U.S began a pre-emptive war against the same Iraqi regime.

The United States dominates this global trade in arms, supplying just under half of all arms exports in 2001, roughly two and a half times more than the second- and third-largest suppliers. US weapons sales help outfit non-democratic regimes, soldiers who commit gross human rights abuses against their fellow citizens and citizens of other countries, and forces in unstable regions on the verge of, in the middle of, or recovering from conflict. This encourages other regimes in developing countries to spend their money on arms rather than on badly needed healthcare and education for their people.

The various branches of the armed forces — Air Force, Army, Marine Corps, Navy — have powerful lobbies working to make sure they get their pet projects funded, and military contractors also lobby to ensure they get the contracts for those projects. Military contractors are among the biggest contributors to members of Congress, and other groups with an interest in nonmilitary spending in the discretionary budget do not have similarly powerful advocates to push for their programs. Military contractors have also been expanding their involvement with the US government in recent years, moving more heavily into NASA and into welfare administration as part of an over-all drive to privatize previously public functions.

PI POINTER

Lockheed Martin, known for racking up cost overruns while building weapons, has found another way to access government resources, taking on contracts for implementing welfare programs, enforcing child support, and collecting government data.

A variety of corporate subsidies cost taxpayers hundreds of billions of dollars and often go to increase the profit margin of corporations or augment CEO compensation rather than create new jobs. As we saw in Chapter 2, there are special tax breaks in the income side of the budget that help corporations retain more of their profits. On the expense side of the budget there are more than 120 programs to help corporations.

One example Ralph Nader pointed to, in testimony to the House Budget Committee on corporate welfare, is the use of government research and development funds to support drug and pharmaceutical companies. The drug Taxol, which is used to treat ovarian cancer, was developed thanks to a grant of $31 million from the National Institutes of Health, which supported research right through the clinical testing process. The formula was then given to the Bristol-Myers Squibb company for no charge. No royalties were paid to the taxpayer, and there was no restraint on the price Bristol-Myers Squibb could charge for the drug. In 2002, Attorney General Richard Blumenthal of Connecticut filed an antitrust suit, charging the company with manipulating the US patent office and blocking generic production of the drug. Blumenthal argued that "this medicine is a necessity, not a luxury, for thousands of people with cancer — a condition that Bristol-Myers exploited financially through flagrant, illegal misconduct."[2]

The price of Taxol now runs between $6,000 and $10,000 per patient for a series of treatments. Patients, who are also taxpayers, pay this amount for a drug they funded through their taxes. If the patients can't pay, they go on Medicaid, and other taxpayers pay for the drug again at the other end of the cycle. Bristol-Myers Squibb's sales of Taxol have totaled at least $5.4 billion since 1998.

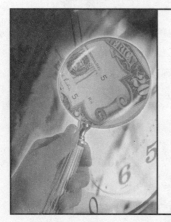

PI POINTER

Every major industry has received research and development money from the government. This contradicts the myth that there is free enterprise in our economy.

Another example is the savings and loan bailout, which will cost taxpayers close to $500 billion by the time it is paid out in the year 2020. Ronal Reagan deregulated the troubled savings and loan industry, which led to a crisis that came to a head during the George Bush Sr. administration. Taxpayers are still footing the bill.

Accounting and National Expenses

In Chapter 2 we saw that *how* the income side of the budget is constructed and *how* the accounts are kept and made available to the public are important parts of the policy impact of the budget. This is true also on the expense side of the budget. Two examples of how government accounting and accountability have failed, and how this could affect policy, are provided by military spending and Native American trust funds.

First, let's look at the accounting issues with respect to the military budget. As mentioned earlier, the military takes over half of the discretionary spending in the budget each year, which is now over $400 billion a year. Since 1980, the president and the military have made the case to Congress that more money is needed for national defense. However, according to the Council for a Livable World, the Pentagon's problem is not a lack of money but "chaotic accounting and mismanagement that leaves the Pentagon in the dark about what it is buying, what assets it holds and what it needs for the future." The defense department's own Inspector General's office found $1.1 trillion in bookkeeping entries that could not be tracked or justified.

The Government Accountability Office (GAO), the investigative arm of Congress, also reported that no major part of the defense department's operations could pass the test of an independent financial audit. The GAO report stated:

> The Department of Defense's (DOD) financial manage-
> ment deficiencies, taken together, continue to represent
> the single largest obstacle to achieving an unqualified
> opinion on the US government's consolidated financial
> statements. For example, to date, none of the military
> services has passed the test of an independent financial
> audit because of pervasive weaknesses in internal control,
> processes, and fundamentally flawed business systems ...
> The department continues to rely on a reported 4,000
> or more fundamentally flawed finance, logistics, per-
> sonnel, acquisition, and other management information
> systems to gather the data needed to support day-to-
> day management decision making and reporting. These
> systems ... evolved into the overly complex and error-
> prone operation — vulnerable to fraud, waste, and abuse
> — that exists today.[3]

Senators overseeing the effort to clarify defense department account-
ing pointed out that for seven fiscal years they have been unable to audit the department because of the chaos. Although the defense department has agreed to an audit in fiscal year 2007, the senators and GAO see no evidence that it will be ready for such scrutiny.

What is the consequence of this lack of a money trail? Congress does not know how much is being spent on many Pentagon programs and so cannot fulfill its constitutional obligation to oversee

government spending. Because of the confusion over its finances, the Pentagon can and does shift funds from one account to another and spends money on projects that Congress has not approved. However, under the Constitution, money appropriated for a specific program cannot be spent on something else. Though most Americans have heard nothing about this fundamental mishandling of public monies, it surely ranks as one of the largest consumer frauds in history.

PI POINTER

If money has not been spent in a program, it is supposed to be rescinded, or given back, to the government. If the Pentagon gave back what it hasn't spent (or what hasn't been accounted for) we could protect Social Security without new taxes.

Some members of Congress have spoken out about this and recognize the enormity of this issue. Sen. Charles Grassley (R-IA) said on the floor of the Senate in February 2001: "If the Pentagon does not know what it owns and spends, then how does the Pentagon know if it needs more money? Ramping up the Pentagon budget when the books are a mess is highly questionable at best. To some it might seem crazy." Of course this was before the attack of September 11, 2001, and the Iraq War. Since then, this kind of critique has been muted.

The second example of the challenges the government faces in tracking money is its handling of Native American trust fund accounts. This story goes back to 1887, when Indian land holdings were broken into small parcels, and the US government took charge of the parcels for individual Native Americans. The government, as trustee, was to collect revenues generated by mining, oil, timber, grazing, and other interests. It would then distribute the money to the heirs of the original landholders. Currently the Department of the Interior (DOI) holds millions of acres of land in trust — originally it held 50 million acres, but that is now down to 11 million. From the beginning the trust fund was mismanaged, and Native American sources estimate that more than $100 billion in royalties may be due 500,000 individuals. It is not clear where the money has gone.

Eloise Cobell, a Blackfeet woman, filed one of the largest class-action suits in US history in 1996. The purpose of the suit was to force the US government to account for the billions of dollars in the individual accounts. Her suit has been in process since then and is now called *Cobell vs. Norton*. US District Court judge Royce Lamberth charged Gale Norton, secretary of the DOI at the time, with civil contempt, stating that she committed a fraud on the court and undermined the public trust by lying about her department's efforts to address the problem.

PI POINTER

One of the responsibilities the government assumed as legal trustee when it took Indian lands was to provide basic social, medical, and educational services for tribal members. However, national investments in key programs for tribes, such as child healthcare, have been declining in the last few decades.

Cobell is a founder and current chair of the Blackfeet National Bank. She has been a proponent of economic development as a path to financial independence for Native Americans. Ms. Cobell remembers as a little girl hearing her relatives grumble about Indian trust accounts poorly maintained by the US government. When she became treasurer of the Blackfeet Nation years later, she questioned Bureau of Indian Affairs officials about the chaotic state of the accounts. "They said, 'Oh, you don't know how to read the reports,' and I sat down," she said "I think they were trying to embarrass me, but it did the opposite — it made me mad."[4]

Lamberth ordered the Interior Department to let landowners know about possible sales, and as of 2005, according to the website for the case, court rulings point to an ultimate resolution that could result in tens of billions of dollars going to trust beneficiaries. Cobell said in response to previous court rulings: "For more than a century, the U.S. government has sold our land out from under us — without consent, without appraisal and without informing us of our rights as trust beneficiaries. That ends today."[5]

Is the National Government Too Big?

In recent years, residents of the United States have been bombarded with the assertion that the government is too big. The real issue is not big government or small government — the government is about the same size as it was 20 years ago — but what the government's resources will be used for and how we will achieve a national consensus on how we want to spend public resources. In fact, though the US is the wealthiest country, we have the lowest amount of public spending of all the major industrialized nations.

❖

CHAPTER 4

Debt or Surplus?

THE NATIONAL BUDGET CONSISTS OF income to the government and expenses the government pays, but this alone does not provide a complete picture of the use of national resources. As PIs, we also need to examine the deeper relationship between income and expenses, since that relationship affects the money in our pocketbooks as well as the funds in the government's books. In any given year the interaction between income and expenses can result in one of three things: a balanced budget (equal amounts of income and expenses), a deficit (more expenses than income), or a surplus (more income than expenses).

Another way to understand this is to picture the rivers of money flowing in and out of Washington, with the national budget providing a structure for those flows. Money flows into the government through several streams created by tax and other revenue laws. The money received then flows out to government programs and purchases based on the spending decisions of Congress. So if the budget is balanced, the in-flowing river is the same size as the out-flowing river. If the budget is in deficit, the in-flowing river is smaller than the streams flowing out, and if the budget is in surplus, the out-flowing river equals the in-flowing streams, but there is also a reservoir that the government can release funds from when necessary, or the money can be directed into new channels.

This relationship between in-flow and out-flow fluctuates depending on politics and the dynamics of the budgeting process in any given year. These fluctuations can be seen in our recent history: in 2000 there was a budget surplus; in 2005 the budget is generating huge yearly deficits and will probably continue to do so for many years to come unless there are major policy changes. Government spending is such a large part of the overall US economy that the budget has an effect on how things are going economically for everyone in the country whether it runs a deficit or surplus, or is balanced.

Why does the US government go into debt? There are usually a number of reasons, and it can be hard to pinpoint only one cause of indebtedness at any given time. The following are some of the common reasons:

❖ To finance war and war preparedness

❖ To cover new spending or emergency spending

❖ To create jobs and/or income support during a time of high unemployment and economic downturn

❖ To stimulate the economy overall

Government debt is not necessarily a bad thing. It is always important to look at the larger context for any debt and the purpose for which it is used. Just as you could go into debt to gamble at a casino or to send your child to college, the government can go into debt to put more money in the pockets of the wealthy or to invest in affordable housing. Many economists believe that the country should be going into debt, if necessary, to invest in education, housing, and other long-term needs of the nation. If deficit spending helps to create jobs during an economic downturn, this serves to strengthen the economy. However, if the debt increases too much without an accompanying plan for debt reduction, it can harm the economy and endanger key government programs in the long run.

The government has to make decisions about how to handle its debt, just as you do. You may be in debt with medical bills, a mortgage, car payments, a college loan, credit card debt, loans from family and friends, other bank loans, or business loans. In that case, part of your expense budget will go to pay down the debt, or at least to cover any interest that is being charged. If you have more income than expenses, you will have to decide what to do with the surplus: reduce some of your debt, purchase needed things, and/or save or invest the money. The government faces the same decisions.

Just as debt is not necessarily bad, a surplus or a balanced budget is not necessarily good. The impact of a surplus or a balanced budget depends on the overall budget picture, whether the needs of most citizens are being met, and the values that are being reflected in the budget policies. If a surplus is created by reducing spending on programs for low-income Americans and allowing corporations to pay low taxes, the surplus comes at too high a price. During the 1990s, when many conservative politicians argued for a balanced budget — even going so far as proposing a constitutional amendment to require a balanced budget each year — their surface motivation was responsible stewardship of national resources, including not saddling future generations with too much debt. When you took a deeper look at the policies this group supported, however, you could see that its definition of "responsible" was connected to holding social spending down, while allowing large military budgets and tax breaks for the wealthy and corporations. (This strategy of advocating for a constitutional amendment requiring a balanced budget was revived by a group of conservatives in 2004.)

One way that debt — no matter what its purpose — has a direct and immediate impact on taxpayers and the budget each year is through the interest on the debt. Interest payments are a huge direct cost to taxpayers each year, taking at least one in every seven dollars in the national budget. This is a mandatory expense — the government must pay the full amount of interest due each year. In the last five years, over $2 trillion has been spent on interest payments. This amount is equivalent to the entire annual national budget.

History of the National Debt

The second clause of Article I of the US Constitution grants Congress the power "to borrow money on the credit of the United States." Due to the general nature of this permission, Congress can borrow for any purpose, borrow as much as it wants, choose any lender, and make the loan on any terms. In 1847 Congress passed permanent legislation that authorized, in advance, payment of whatever interest is owed on the national debt. This is in effect a blank check for payment of interest, since it says that each year the interest will be paid no matter what else may be going on in that year.

For most of the nation's history, increases in the national debt have been the result of either wars or economic downturns. Government decisions to go to war necessitated major increases in military spending, while economic downturns reduced federal tax revenues from businesses and individuals and often increased federal payouts to economically stressed individuals. The government generated deficits during the War of 1812, the recession of 1837, the Civil War, the depression of the 1890s, and World War I. Each time the war ended or the economy began to grow, the government followed its deficits with budget surpluses, with which it paid down the debt.

The Great Depression, which came on the heels of the Wall Street stock-market crash of 1929, was a terrible downturn in the economy that affected millions through unemployment, farm and business bankruptcies, and collapsing financial institutions. The Great Depression lasted over a decade and, combined with the spending on President Franklin D. Roosevelt's New Deal, contributed to large deficits from 1931 to the end of the decade.

It was followed by World War II, which created unprecedented deficits. After World War II the federal budget deficit rose in most years, including during the Korean War and the Vietnam War. After several years of large deficits during the Reagan presidency, there was a steady decline in deficits under the Clinton administration. For four years, from 1998 to 2001, there were surpluses. Since George W. Bush took office in 2001, he has created the largest deficits in the last 50 years.

Budget surpluses outnumbered budget deficits prior to 1930. Since World War II, however, budget surpluses have been a rarity.

What is the National Debt?

The national debt — known in the official budget as the gross federal debt — is the accumulation of deficits, minus any surpluses. In any given year, the government may not have enough cash to cover its expenses — in other words it runs a deficit. So the government borrows the money to cover the expenses for that year, which adds to the debt. If there is a surplus in a given year, it is subtracted from the debt

The national debt is currently $7.3 trillion. This is over three times the entire annual budget.

There are two different components to the gross federal debt. One part is known as debt held by the public, which was $4.3 trillion in 2004. In this case "public" means non-government, and it distinguishes money owed to people and institutions outside the government from

PI POINTER

If you had 7.3 trillion dollar bills, the amount of the US national debt, and laid them end to end, they would stretch from the Earth to the sun … four times.

the money owed internally to the trust funds (see the next paragraph). The government borrows from banks and other financial institutions, state and local governments, private pension plans, corporations, foreign investors, and private bondholders, including members of the US public who buy savings bonds.

The other part of the gross federal debt is called intragovernmental holdings. It is the amount lent to the government by what is known in the budget as the federal trust funds. The major trust funds are Social Security and Medicare. Payroll taxes provide the money for these funds each year (remember FICA from Chapter 1), and any surplus left over after the Social Security and Medicare benefits are paid out that year must be lent to the government. The trust funds are required by law to invest in US bonds when they have a surplus. In this way the government borrows from itself. Intragovernmental holdings amounted to $3 trillion in 2004.

As accumulated deficits (minus any surpluses) add up to the national debt, Congress needs to have permission to keep raising the debt. The "debt ceiling," a law that must be passed by Congress and signed by the president, sets Washington's borrowing limit. In effect, Congress keeps increasing its own line of credit. When the national debt reaches the amount set by the debt ceiling, Congress must pass a new debt ceiling law so that the government can continue to pay expenses that are not covered by income in a given year. Congress has tried for decades to set a finite ceiling on the national debt, but these attempts have failed. Members of Congress just keep pushing the debt ceiling higher.

Government Borrowing

So we now know that the government has to borrow money to cover its deficits, but what does it mean for the national government to borrow money? It means the government has to sell bonds to the following buyers:

❖ Banks and financial institutions

❖ Corporations

❖ Individuals (including you and me, if we choose)

❖ Foreign investors

❖ State and local governments.

These groups lend their money to the government, and the government pays them interest each year from money it has collected in taxes.

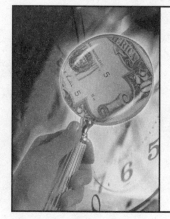

PI POINTER

Even though it is called "debt held by the public," a lot of the debt is held by large financial institutions.

Let's say you purchase a bond from the government (called a savings bond). The government takes your money as a loan. In return it gives you a note that says it promises to pay a specific amount of interest for a specific amount of time on the money you lent. It also promises to repay the principal on the maturity date (the date the bond expires). While the total amount of interest paid on bonds must be recorded in each annual budget as an expense, repayments of principal amounts are considered financing costs and are accounted for outside of the budget.

The groups that lend money to the government, listed in order of the percentage of the debt they hold, are shown in Figure 4.1.

Holders of US Government Public Debt

by percentage

Foreign entities and investors	35 percent
Corporations and insurance companies	24 percent
Federal reserve banks	15 percent
State and local governments	13 percent
Private individuals	12 percent

Note: This table includes only debt held by the public, and not the intragovernmental holdings, which is what the government owes itself.
Source: Joint Economic Committee, US Congress, 2001.

figure 4.1

The national debt is what some people call an internal debt, a debt owed to the "owners" of the debt — the public — so that it really represents an asset for the country as a whole. In other words, the debt on the government's books is cash in someone's pocket. Some of the interest payments currently go to banks and financial institutions, and some makes up part of the income of millions of individuals and businesses in the United States.

This view of the debt as an internal debt has become increasingly less accurate. Before the Reagan administration came to office, the United States was a creditor nation, meaning that other nations owed more to us than we owed to them. However, in a few short years we became a debtor nation as the government was forced to borrow more and more from foreign sources to finance the huge national debt. Most of the debt to foreigners is owned by the central banks of other countries. Japan and China are currently the leading investors, followed by Taiwan and South Korea. They invest in the United States for reasons that have to do with their currencies and their internal needs and politics, and these can change.

Everyone in the United States should be concerned about the amount of the debt held by investors outside the country. The danger of having so much of our debt tied up in this fashion is obvious: if conditions change for the major foreign investors and they decide to call on the US government to repay their loans, we could find it difficult to meet our obligations to them and/or to find enough new investors to meet our needs for credit. If enough foreign investors lost confidence in the US economy, it could threaten the value of US currency and cause an economic crisis. According to William Greider, who has written extensively about international finance, "history suggests ... the creditor nations will eventually assert their leverage over the United States, however reluctantly. That critical juncture is likely to arrive either because the American debt burden has become so great that additional lending would be too risky or because the creditor nations want to jerk Washington's chain, perhaps to head off reckless new adventures."[1]

PI POINTER

More and more of the national debt — over 30 percent — is being purchased by other countries and by investors from outside the US. This is like playing roulette with our economic future.

The Impact of the National Debt

Deficits — and the national debt — are created year by year, policy by policy, budget cycle by budget cycle. As noted above, there are many reasons the government creates deficits, all of which may be totally justified at the time. One example is World War II. Although expenses for the massive war effort produced high levels of debt, it also helped pull the country out of the Great Depression.

Depending on the overall dynamics of the economy, being in deficit, or "deficit spending" as it is sometimes called, can have a positive effect on the economy. Whenever the government spends, it helps to put money in circulation and can lead to an increase in employment. This creates a ripple effect, as people have more resources with which to buy goods, and that helps local businesses to grow, hiring more workers and buying more goods. If the government directly purchases goods, as it does during a war or when preparing for a war, military industries get a boost, which can also help the economy grow.

However, it has been shown that money invested in the social sector tends to create more jobs. Also, women make up a larger proportion of workers in nonmilitary industries, so money spent in other sectors benefits them more. The amount the government has spent on wars and the military in the last 50 years would have stimulated the economy just as well if it had been spent on nonmilitary programs, and it may have been more beneficial for women. As PIs we always need to look at what the deficit is being created for.

A study by Employment Research Associates in the 1980s showed that if the money spent on the military build-up between 1981 and 1985 had been spent on civilian economic activities, 1,146,000 more jobs would have been generated. Over 80 percent of the jobs lost to military spending would have gone to women.

When the deficit gets too large, it can affect the general economy in a negative way. Large-scale borrowing takes up a lot of room in the economy and can contribute to less capital being available to invest in the private sector. When the government borrows to finance debt, it increases the competition for credit and can drive up interest rates, which in turn costs the government, and everyone else who borrows, more in interest payments. Higher interest rates can slow economic growth because they make it more expensive to borrow money available for businesses to expand and create jobs.

Another impact of the debt is that interest payments have taken up an increasingly large share of annual budget expenses since the early 1980s. This ties up money that could be spent on other needed things, and it means less money is available to help tide people over when the economy takes a downturn. In any given budget year, once interest and entitlements — those programs that must be covered — are paid, only a third of the budget is left for all the other programs and functions of the budget.

To look at other impacts of the national debt, we need to return to the history of deficits. The recent history of budget deficits goes back to the policies of the Reagan administration in the early 1980s. The government of the time decided to greatly increase military spending, reduce taxes for the wealthy and corporations, and cut social spending, which resulted in large deficits. These policies worked synergistically: the tax cuts insured that there would not be enough money to cover the increased military spending, and both policies transferred wealth to the rich and to military contractors and other corporations. In turn, the huge deficits were used as the pretext for cutting programs on the domestic (or nonmilitary) side of the budget and for reducing the government's role in moving the economy toward greater economic equity for all.

The deficits that were created under the Reagan administration also spawned legislation that influenced the annual budgets for many years to come. In an attempt to gain control of the debt, Congress passed the Balanced Budget and Emergency Deficit Control Act of 1985, known as the Gramm-Rudman-Hollings bill (GRH) after Phil Gramm (R-TX), Warren Rudman (R-NH), and Ernest Hollings (D-SC). This law established a schedule for gradually reducing the annual deficits to zero by fiscal 1991, required the president to follow this schedule when submitting the budget, and required Congress to follow specific deficit-reduction targets when it passed the budget resolution. If the president and Congress failed to adhere to the deficit-reduction schedule, the statute provided for the comptroller general to make automatic across-the-board spending cuts, with half the reductions coming from military programs.

In 1986 the Supreme Court struck down this automatic budget-cutting mechanism as a violation of the Constitution's doctrine of the separation of powers. A revised version of the act was passed in 1987, but it failed to reduce the debt because Congress kept increasing the debt ceiling.

The influence of GRH continued for many years, however, and fostered an approach to reducing yearly deficits that focused on cutting or limiting spending on every program instead of looking at the value of programs. A 1990 revision of the act explicitly changed the focus from deficit reduction to spending control. In addition, although military spending was supposed to take 50 percent of the cuts, military programs were many times exempted from cuts while programs that benefited low-income Americans were cut.

According to the late Daniel Patrick Moynihan, a New York Democrat who was a senator for 24 years, from 1976 until 2000, David Stockman, budget director under President Reagan, coined the term the "strategic deficit" — that is, the deficit as political weapon. Moynihan said the budget director had told him privately that the administration's plan was to have a strategic deficit. "That gives you an argument for cutting back programs that really weren't desired and ... an argument against establishing new programs you didn't really want."[2]

Who Benefits from the Debt?

We cannot understand the impact of the debt without looking at the issue of interest. In order to fully understand the "cost" of the debt, we need to look at who benefits from the interest payments on the debt. These interest payments constitute a huge transfer of wealth from working-class and middle-income people to a group made up mostly of corporations, banks, insurance companies, and wealthy investors, many of them from other countries.

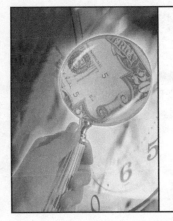

PI POINTER

Deficits can be policy tools in themselves, not just the results of tax cuts or spending excesses. David Stockman, budget director under Reagan, used the term "strategic deficit" to describe the use of deficits to force program cuts and stop new programs from being created.

As Magrit Kennedy, an architect and urban planner with an interest in currency and money issues, has written: "Interest is a hidden redistribution mechanism that constantly shuttles money from those who have less money than they need to those who have more money than they need." Interest payments on the national debt are obviously part of this redistribution mechanism.

Kennedy also points out that if you compare interest paid and interest gained in terms of income groups, the bottom 80 percent of income earners pay out much more in interest over their lifetimes than they receive, whereas the top 20 percent receive much more in interest than they pay out. If you have substantial savings or investments, you will benefit as interest rates go up. If you have lots of debt, which is subject to the variation in interest rates, you will be penalized if interest rates go up.

PI POINTER

Taxpayers pay the interest when the government borrows, but they may or may not benefit from the debt. That depends on what the borrowed money is being used for.

Although it is hard to measure the distribution of wealth and difficult to tell exactly how much women have, we do know that women own far less property and far fewer stocks, bonds, and other financial assets than men. This means that most women are caught in that place where they will pay out more interest over the course of their life — not just in relation to taxes — than they will ever get back. Women of color are disproportionately denied benefits from large interest payments on the federal debt. White men continue to monopolize wealth ownership, and white families have median net worth 20 times greater than families of color. Many married women benefit from interest income if their and their spouse's combined assets are substantial. But although they may benefit financially from this situation, it does not mean they control the assets or the income from the interest.

Another way that people with wealth benefit from the debt is by supporting public policies that ensure paying interest on the debt crowds out other types of spending, particularly social spending. These policies negatively affect the economic standing and options of most women because social programs constitute a vital social safety net for women, particularly those supporting children on their own. In addition, when spending is cut in the public sphere, where women are more often employed, women lose jobs.

Supporting interest payment over social spending is one of the ways a deficit can be used strategically, as discussed above. Discretionary spending — which is allocated in the yearly budget process — makes up only 39 percent of the total budget. This means that any program other than entitlements like Social Security, Medicare, and interest payments is competing for a very small slice of the pie.

Surpluses

When the cash revenues received by the federal government in a given time period exceed the cash outlays in that same time period, the result is a surplus. There is no clear consensus about what the government should use a surplus for, either in good economic times or bad. If there is a possibility of an economic downturn, Congress could use the budget surplus to cut taxes, to pay off part of the national debt, or to increase spending (i.e., to make investments).

After 28 consecutive years of deficits, the government had a surplus from 1998 to 2001. In 2001, when President George W. Bush took office, there was a surplus of $281 billion. Within three years, the national budget had a deficit of $400 billion, and larger ones were coming.

The public did not have a chance to indicate what it thought should be done with the surpluses in the late 1990s because they were gone so quickly. The last time there had been a surplus before that was in fiscal year 1969, when the economic and political situation in the United States was totally different. The $3.2 billion surplus in 1969 was used to create a new program — General Revenue Sharing — that sent the money back to the states to be used as they and local governments wanted.

When it looked like the late-1990s surplus would be around for many years to come, the congressional politics became very complicated. Budget legislation that was in effect in 1998 made it impossible for the surplus to be used for anything other than debt reduction. However, several different groups emerged in Congress with proposals for how the surplus could be used, including the following suggestions:

❖ Continue spending cuts

❖ Create tax cuts

❖ Increase spending

❖ Increase spending on certain programs

❖ Reduce the national debt

❖ Hold off on doing anything until politicians could agree on a long-term solution to the Social Security problem.

Most members of Congress were frustrated that there were not enough votes to waive the budget process restrictions that prevented the surplus being used for anything other than reducing the debt.

Of course, the whole debate around the surplus was ridiculous on one level, since the last 20 years have seen drastic cuts to investments in and spending on the social infrastructure of the country, particularly in programs that affect low-income people. Analyses of the Office of Management and Budget and the Congressional Budget Office have shown that the bulk of the projected surpluses actually came primarily from cuts in discretionary spending — from cuts in these programs. The debt that grew in the 1980s and early 1990s was partly the result of the huge gap in available national resources created by the large military increases and tax breaks for the wealthy and businesses. So at least part of the surplus should have been paid back to the community to make up for all those years of lost investment.

The Nation's Balance Sheet

Unlike a business, the government is not required to make a profit to return to stockholders. This means that the "bottom line" of the budget does not have to dictate everything. One advantage of this is that the government can decide to have a positive impact on the economy on behalf of the people by investing in jobs and housing, for example, even if it creates a deficit. The disadvantage of not having to focus on the bottom line is that the government can use public monies to enrich the wealthy and corporations, and it can hurt the economy and key government programs without any accountability.

Because the government is not a business, its decisions do not have to be made in the context of a balance sheet that shows the relationship of assets and liabilities. However, as the "stockholders" of the government, we need to understand this larger picture. We are the owners of these assets, and the people who will pay for the liabilities. (If you want to see the budget presentation of the assets and liabilities of the US government, go to <www.gpoaccess.gov/ usbudget/ fy06/pdf/spec.pdf> and look at Table 13-1.)

What do we see when we look at this informal balance sheet? One of the things that becomes obvious is just how powerful an actor the government is in the US economy. Government assets make up

40 percent of the gross domestic product, the total amount of goods and services produced in a given year. We see that the US government owns a lot of stuff and funds a lot of stuff. We also notice that there is so much debt that the liabilities outweigh the assets. (Transfer payments, including Social Security, are not counted as a liability.)

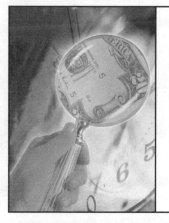

PI POINTER

Women are 51 percent of the owners of national assets — land (a third of the country), buildings, and equipment — yet have little to say about how they are used or maintained.

This balance sheet gives us a reading on our national wealth and also shows us what resources we as citizens own together as a community. We often hear about our huge liability, known as the national debt, but rarely do we hear about our overall national assets. Just as you need to consider your assets and liabilities, along with your income and expenses, to get the full picture of your personal finances, so too, for the country. We must look not only at the national budget, which includes the income and expenses, but also at the national balance sheet, which includes the assets and liabilities. Ever since 1960, government liabilities have exceeded the value of the assets. As pointed out before, if the government is in debt, it is not necessarily a bad thing; it is important to look at why the debt was created and whether it is achieving national objectives that serve all of us.

In the federal budget documents, national wealth is officially defined as the country's assets, not just the assets in the balance sheet connected to the federal budget. The national wealth includes: mortgages; physical assets such as office buildings, equipment, and bombs; vast tracts of land; oil and mineral rights; and the public airwaves. According to the federal government's definition of national wealth, it also includes federal, state, and local investments in education; federal and other research and development; and grants to state and local government. In fiscal year 2000, the national wealth figured this way added up to $78 trillion.

The fact that few people know the overall financial condition of the government means that some of these assets can be manipulated without much public scrutiny.

CHAPTER 5

❖

Who Decides?

I N PREVIOUS CHAPTERS we've seen how money flows into the budget in the form of taxes, how it flows out in spending, and what happens when there is a deficit or a surplus. Now we will look at how the budget is made and who is deciding how to spend public resources. As PIs, we know that how the budget is made will influence its effect on women.

First we will look into the basic steps of the current budget process to see what our elected representatives are required to do to prepare the budget. Then we will investigate the deeper reality behind these steps, the dynamics that illuminate the fundamental questions of democracy and accountability regarding the government's trusteeship of our national resources.

One important thing to remember is that most of the work that Congress does is creating and overseeing the budget in a continuous cycle. "Budgeting is governing," as Pete Domenici (R-NM), the former chairman of the Senate Budget Committee, has said.[1] The congressional historian George B. Galloway wrote that, directly or indirectly, "perhaps nine-tenths of the work of Congress is concerned...with the spending of public money."[2] The Constitution granted the legislative branch of our government the power to tax, spend, and borrow, which gave it tremendous power, especially as the US economy has grown to be the largest in the world.

Because of the decentralized structure of Congress, with various committees dealing with a large number of issues, many members are experts in their area and know nothing about the work other members are doing. Typically, only a handful of budget analysts and experts, policy makers, congressional aides, and administration officials have a grasp of the overall budget or are aware of the impact of budget policy on the US people. Often, members of Congress pass important legislation — including budget legislation — without actually having read it. Politics frequently have more to do with which factions in Congress support a bill than the actual content of the legislation.

There are a few basics to keep in mind about how the national government functions. Congress has two parts or "chambers" — the House of Representatives (in which each state is represented based on population) and the Senate (in which each state has two senators). Most of the work Congress does takes place in committees. There are about 250 committees and subcommittees, each made up of representatives from both parties. Any member of the House or Senate can introduce legislation, which is referred to the appropriate committee. The committees then debate and decide whether to recommend the legislation to the full House and Senate, and members in both chambers vote on this legislation. If both chambers agree to legislation, the president must also agree to it and sign it before it becomes law. The president can veto legislation, and the Congress can override his veto by a two-thirds vote.

PI POINTER

According to the Constitution, any legislation dealing with taxes must originate in the House Ways and Means Committee.

If the Senate and House versions of legislation differ — which is common — representatives of both houses form what is called a "conference committee" to create a compromise between those versions. Both chambers must vote again on the compromise legislation before it has a chance of becoming law. You will often read in the paper or hear on the news that the House or the Senate passed such and such a bill. However, that doesn't mean the bill will become law. It may not be passed by the other house; it may not make it through the conference committee, or may be substantially changed in that process; or, of course, it may end up being vetoed by the president. Most bills follow a very long and circuitous route, and only a few make it to the end. Even budget bills are subject to many changes, and the details are often ironed out in the last days before final passage.

PI POINTER

Your elected representatives are working in committee or subcommittee on something related to the budget. Raising and spending trillions involves every member of Congress.

Entering Budget Territory

The national budget is prepared, along with all other legislation, in the center of Washington, D.C. The city is divided into four quadrants that radiate out from Capitol Hill. The Senate and House of Representatives chambers are both in the Capitol building, while the offices of representatives and senators are located in large buildings around the Capitol — the representatives across from the House side of the Capitol and the senators across from the Senate side. The White House is down the long stretch of mall from the Capitol.

The place where the budget is created is filled with the spirits of the people who built it, who work there, and who lived and live now in the neighborhood. As we consider this place where our resources are collected and spent, we should keep some things in mind about the history and current reality of this budget territory. First, according to the White House Historical Association, slaves provided the bulk of the labor to build the White House, Capitol, and other government buildings, which include some of the key buildings and rooms in which budget decisions are made. Recently discovered public records confirm this use of African American slave labor. For example, US Treasury promissory notes show that slave owners were promised $5 a month for each of their slaves who worked on the construction. These Treasury Department pay slips indicate that more than two thirds of the laborers who worked on the White House and the Capitol were of African descent — 400 slaves and 50 freemen.

In *The Debt: What America Owes to Blacks*, Randall Robinson describes his impressions as he watched tourists in the Capitol rotunda: "The worn and pitted stones on which the tourists stood had doubtless been hauled into position by slaves, for whom the most arduous of tasks were reserved. They had fired and stacked the bricks. They had mixed the mortar. They had sawn the long timbers in hellishly dangerous pits with one slave out of the pit and another in, often nearly buried alive in sawdust."

I emphasize the fact that slaves made up most of the workforce that built the Capitol and the White House because the nation still has not come to terms with the legacy of slavery. There is an economic and social legacy of slavery for the African American community, and for the country as a whole, that continues to this day. It is outlined in Robinson's book.

In addition, the statue on top of the Capitol — called the Statue of Freedom — was cast by slave Philip Reed and assembled and placed atop the Capitol by slaves. On the Architect of the Capitol website, the statue is described as "a classical female figure of Freedom wearing flowing draperies. Her right hand rests upon the hilt of a sheathed sword; her left holds a laurel wreath of victory and the shield of the United States with thirteen stripes. Her helmet is encircled by stars and features a crest composed of an eagle's head, feathers, and talons, a reference to the costume of Native Americans."

This reminds us of another reality we need to be aware of as we think about where the budget is prepared: the systematic wars against, forced dislocations of, and stealing of land from the dozens of Native American tribes that populated North America. The early days of this history are depicted prominently in the Capitol in four reliefs sculpted over each of the rotunda doors: "Landing of the Pilgrims, 1620"; "Conflict of Daniel Boone and the Indians, 1773";

"Preservation of Captain Smith by Pocahontas, 1606"; and "William Penn's Treaty with the Indians, 1682." They were all completed in the 1820s, the decade leading up to the Indian Removal Act of 1830. The Powhatan Nation and the Piscataways were just two of the Maryland and Virginia tribes who had inhabited the area where Washington, DC, now sits. Similar to the unresolved legacy of slavery, there is also an unresolved legacy from the destruction of Native American lives and culture perpetrated by those who came later.

We need to be aware of the government's profound impact on the city in which it is located. The people of Washington, DC, who are predominantly people of color, with 60 percent of the population made up of African Americans, continue to be denied their basic political rights to elected representation and control over their own resources by the US government. The District of Columbia is prohibited from becoming a state, which means that 560,000 people in the US are not allowed to elect a true representative, but only a non-voting "delegate," similar to Puerto Rico or Guam. This delegate can cast votes in committees but is not allowed to vote for legislation on the floor of the House of Representatives, the heart of the legislative power. And because the District of Columbia is not a state, residents have no representation in the Senate.

Residents of DC have also been systematically denied their basic economic rights and are dictated to by members of Congress from around the country. The city's finances are overseen and ultimately controlled by committees in the House and Senate. It was not until

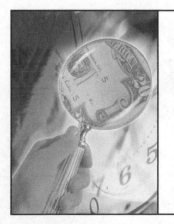

PI POINTER

Many residents of Washington, DC, have worked for decades to achieve full political rights through statehood. They are tired of having taxation without representation — paying hundreds of millions of dollars to the federal government but having no vote in Congress.

the 1960s that residents of DC were allowed to vote for the president, and only in the 1970s did they elect their own mayor and city council for the first time.

Thousands of employees work in the government buildings — as legislative and administrative staff to members of Congress, for committees of Congress, and as cafeteria workers, security personnel, and cleaners. Until 1995 these workers were exempted from all the laws that Congress had passed over the years to protect every other worker in the United States against employment discrimination, age discrimination, unsafe and unhealthy working conditions, and unfair labor practices. On January 23, 1995, President Clinton signed the Congressional Accountability Act, which applied 11 existing employment, civil rights, health, and safety-related statutes and regulations to employees in the legislative branch.

History of the Budget Process

The Constitution does not include any provision requiring a budget. It also does not require the president to make recommendations concerning the revenues and spending of the federal government. Over time, however, a complex and mysterious process has evolved that is now used to approve how the government collects and spends its income.

Until 1921 the federal government operated without a comprehensive presidential budget process. Chairmen of congressional committees started to exercise tremendous control over the business of Congress — and therefore gained control over the taxation and spending process — in the early 20th century. The Budget and Accounting Act of 1921 created a national budget system that required the president to prepare and submit a budget to Congress each year. It also established the Bureau of the Budget (now named the Office of Management and Budget or OMB) to help the president prepare the budget proposal each year and to implement the budget once passed, and established the General Accounting Office (GAO — now the Government Accountability Office) to provide oversight.

The 1946 Legislative Reorganization Act set the foundation for the committee system used today — a key component of producing the budget — which gives the House and Senate their own procedures and allows each committee to set its own rules within those procedures. The Legislative Reorganization Act of 1970 revised committee procedures to provide more transparency and accountability. Provisions of the law "encouraged open committee meetings, required that committees have written rules, required that all committee roll call votes be made public, allowed radio and television coverage of committee hearings, and safeguarded the rights of minority party members on the committee."[3]

In the 1970s, congressional reform activists worked to make the committee system more democratic by challenging the system of seniority. This system allowed the most senior member of a committee to dominate the leadership of the committees, which disproportionately affected the committee's legislation. There were also cases of senior members of Congress heading powerful committees when their health was declining and they were barely able to function.

Standing committees have legislative jurisdiction, and most operate with subcommittees that handle the committee's work in specific areas. Select committees have narrower legislative jurisdiction. Joint committees deal with oversight or housekeeping issues. The chair of each committee and a majority of its members come from the majority party. There are approximately 2,000 staff members to assist committees, and most staff members are controlled by the majority party.

The basic budget process used today and described below was put into place by the Congressional Budget and Impoundment Control Act of 1974. It took 21 months, the attention of five committees in the Senate and the House, and lengthy debate in both chambers of Congress to pass it. The act was designed to streamline the budget process and give more power to committees — the budget committees in particular — and less to powerful individual leaders of Congress. It also created the Congressional Budget Office (CBO) to assist the House and Senate budget committees (also created by this act) with timely analyses and data for economic and budget decisions. There were major changes to the act in 1985, 1987, 1990, and 1993 in conjunction with legislation establishing and extending the Gramm-Rudman-Hollings Act and the Budget Enforcement Act. Additionally, some rules of the congressional budget process have been incorporated into or augmented by the standing rules of the House and Senate.

The Budget Train

In this section I will outline the current budget process that the president and Congress are required to follow. Then we will look at some of the pressures on this system. The grunt work of preparing and monitoring the budget is done in the subcommittees and committees of the House and Senate, and your representative and senators sit on some of these bodies. It is there that they can become experts on certain budget issues and can also influence (depending on the politics in their committee) whether programs are funded (or not) and how much money they receive. They can also vote for the budget on the floor of the House and Senate, but by then decisions have usually been made and the compromises hammered out.

We are going to look at the budget process as if it were a series of stops for the budget train. This train can drop off and pick up information, decisions, and political realities, taking them from one stop to another. Sometimes the train has to rush back and forth between stops, and sometimes it gets stalled altogether at a stop. In the end, though, all of these stops have to be visited because if the budget is to pass and be signed by the president, it has to have all the right cargo.

Stop 1: The White House

The president proposes a budget for the coming fiscal year. (The federal fiscal year starts October 1 and runs through September 30.) This budget has been prepared over the previous year by the president's budget office, known as the Office of Management and Budget. OMB staff keep track of all income and expenditures for the overall budget and for each government agency. Then OMB puts together a publication called *Budget of the US Government*, which consists of several volumes. This book includes not only the proposal for the next fiscal year's budget, but also many pieces of information including historical tables of all the things the government has funded since 1948.

The president releases the budget proposal in early February, shortly after the annual State of the Union speech — an address to a joint session of the House and the Senate that is broadcast live to the country — in late January. This allows the president to highlight in that speech any major initiatives or changes in budget policies.

PI POINTER

The State of the Union speech is really a declaration of presidential intentions. The congressional budget process reveals which of those intentions will become national policy.

Stop 2: The Budget Committees

Congress uses the president's budget as a starting point, but the budget committee in the Senate and its counterpart in the House will produce their own proposals, known as budget resolutions, that may or may not conform to what the president wants. The budget resolutions set out the basic overall priorities for the next fiscal year and several years to come. They are supposed to be finalized by April 15, but are not always ready by then.

The budget resolutions set the broad framework for the budget, including the following details:

❖ Total revenues

❖ Total new spending for programs (mandatory and discretionary spending)

❖ Total loan obligations

❖ The amount of the deficit or surplus

❖ The debt limit.

The figures in the budget resolutions are binding, which means the committees that put together the details of the budget have to stay within their limits. However, the budget resolutions are not laws; they cannot be signed or vetoed by the president, and no money can be raised or spent as a result of them.

A vital part of the budget resolutions is Congress's agreement on "spending allocations," which are the limits on the amount of money that can be spent on discretionary programs (as opposed to entitlements like Medicare and Social Security) during the coming fiscal year. (There are also projections of spending limits for at least the next five fiscal years.) After the budget committees in the House and the Senate have finalized their budget resolutions, a conference committee — made up of members of both the House and Senate — takes the two versions and produces the final budget resolution, known as the concurrent budget resolution, which both houses approve. This means both House and Senate are working within the same framework as they iron out the details of the budget. (To see a concurrent budget resolution, go to <http://frwebgate.access.gpo.gov/ cgi-bin/get-doc.cgi?dbname=109_cong_bills&docid=f:hc95rh.txt.pdf>.)

Stop 3: Authorization Subcommittees

There are two main components of the Congressional budget process — authorization and appropriation. Authorization is an act of Congress that establishes, or continues the operation of, a federal agency or program An appropriation is an act of Congress that provides the legal authority for federal agencies to make payments for specific things (i.e., administration or programs) — in other words, to spend federal money. The authorization process sets a ceiling on the amount of money that can be spent on a particular program.

No appropriation is supposed to be passed without an authorization, but this rule is often waived. Although technically the authorization component of the budget process takes place "first," in reality authorization and appropriations subcommittees and committees are often meeting at the same time. This is where the budget train may end up shuttling furiously back and forth between stops. Most of the committees of Congress are the authorizing committees; they are grouped under broad program areas and are named for those program areas (they are not actually called authorization committees). Each chamber has one large appropriations committee, which is called an appropriation committee.

Some authorizations are "permanent" (i.e., Social Security and other entitlements) and do not go through the appropriations process. In addition, some spending is funded directly by the authorization committees. The two thirds of spending that is not funded by appropriations bills is called direct spending. This includes Social Security, Medicare, and federal employee retirement payments. Medicaid and some veterans' programs are funded through the annual appropriations process even though they are entitlements.

The authorization subcommittees make recommendations to the authorization committees. This is one point at which input and lobbying from interested organizations — both nonprofit and business groups or individuals — can influence the fate or funding level of a program.

PI POINTER

Although entitlements like Social Security are referred to as "permanent," we must remember that nothing is permanent in government. Anything can be changed through legislation. But permanent programs tend not to change from year to year.

Stop 4: Authorization Committees

The authorization committees in both the House and Senate determine funding levels for programs (based on the recommendations of the subcommittees) and pass authorizing legislation. This allows for the next step: deciding on appropriations for each authorized program.

Stop 5: Appropriations Subcommittees

Once the overall targets are adopted in the budget resolution, the subcommittees of the large appropriations committees in both the House and the Senate propose how much they want to spend on specific programs. The House and Senate appropriations committees each have 13 subcommittees. Every program that is funded each year comes under one of the subcommittees. These 13 subcommittees do not correspond exactly to the budget functions that provide the organizing structure for the president's budget proposal.

The 13 appropriations subcommittees draft legislation that allocates funds to government agencies within their jurisdictions. These subcommittees are responsible for reviewing the president's budget request, hearing testimony from government officials, and drafting the spending plans for the coming fiscal year. Once they are finished, they pass their recommendations on to the full House or Senate appropriations committees, which review and modify the bills and forward them to the floor for consideration.

The appropriations subcommittees are another point where inter-

PI POINTER

Appropriations subcommittees and committees decide on funding for human needs programs, but they are subject to little scrutiny. Do you know what your representative and senators do when they are in Washington?

est groups and business lobbyists can make their views heard on funding for specific programs. They can provide written testimony, present testimony at hearings, and directly lobby members of the subcommittees.

Stop 6: Appropriations Committees

After the appropriations subcommittees "report out" their bills, the appropriations committees consider each one, make any changes they want to within the overall budget resolution guidelines, and then pass them along to the House and Senate chambers. Thirteen appropriations bills are then put together in the following areas:

- ❖ Agriculture
- ❖ Commerce/Justice/State
- ❖ Defense
- ❖ District of Columbia
- ❖ Energy and Water
- ❖ Foreign Operations
- ❖ Homeland Security

❖ Interior

❖ Labor/Health and Human Services/Education

❖ Legislative Branch

❖ Military Construction

❖ Transportation/Treasury/Postal Service

❖ Veterans Affairs/Housing and Urban Development.

If separate bills are not passed, they are put together in what is called an omnibus bill.

The Budget Act allows the appropriations committees from May 15 until June 10 to finalize the 13 appropriations bills or the omnibus bills.

Stops 7 and 8: The House and Senate Chambers

Each of the 13 appropriations bills has to be approved by votes in the House and Senate. The bills have to be passed by a majority of both houses of Congress.

Stop 9: Conference Committee

If, as usually happens, all the bills are not passed, they are then sent to conference committees to come to compromise. After the conference committees have reached an agreement, they forward the new bills to the House and Senate, which still must approve them by a majority vote.

Stop 10: Budget Committees

At this point the budget committees (one in the House and one in the Senate) compare the expenses set out in the appropriations bills to the revenues the government expects to receive in the next fiscal year and "reconciles" them. This means they make sure all the spending and tax legislation relating to that year's budget (including entitlements) conforms to the budget resolution. At this point, appropriations committees may have to have to redo their bills to stay within the limits. When the appropriations committees have made their changes, the budget committees report the results in what is known as the "reconciliation bill." This is supposed to happen by September 30.

The two budget committees meet in a conference committee to come to a compromise, which then must be signed by the president.

Stop 11: The White House

If the president signs the reconciliation bill, the government's spending is set for the fiscal year. Under law, the president can veto the reconciliation bill. If he does, and Congress overrides his veto by a two-thirds majority, the bill becomes law anyway. If the president vetoes the bill and Congress can't override his veto, then the conference committees have to reconvene and do some more work on it.

When the process goes as planned, all 13 spending bills will have been signed by the president and become law by October 1, the start of the new fiscal year. The direct spending portion of the budget will have been determined through the authorization process, as noted above.

After all this, your money is now available to be spent on all those programs!

Unscheduled Stops

It sometimes happens that the train stops before it's supposed to, and Congress does not pass all the appropriations bills in time for the start of the fiscal year. In that case, Congress must pass a continuing resolution that temporarily funds programs, usually at the current levels of funding, until the final budget is passed. If Congress cannot agree on a continuing resolution, or if the president vetoes it, then government spending on these programs has to stop. This has happened five times since 1981.

In addition to interrupting the work of hundreds of thousand of government employees, government shutdowns cost the American people. For example, when the government shut down for six days in 1995, the Clinton administration estimated the financial cost included over $400 million in lost income to the Treasury, $800 million in home loans to low- and moderate-income families delayed, and two million visitors turned away from national parks.[4]

The Budget and Democracy

When we look at the actors at each stop of the budget train, what do we see? They are mostly white males sitting around tables, dividing up our resources. They have developed rules and procedures and processes for making these resource allocations. These rules, procedures, and processes can be, and have been, changed many times according to political pressures within Congress for more power sharing. However, the rules and procedures have not resulted in a truly transparent or democratic process. As we just saw, the process can even hold the country hostage when political conflicts lead to a government shutdown.

In order for the budget process to be more democratic, it needs to be "transparent." Transparency means that the rules, procedures, processes, and final product — the budget — must be accessible and easy for anyone to understand. The question of transparency leads directly to the question of democracy. The process is democratic only if it is truly participatory — decision makers must represent and be responsive to the people, and the process must be free from pressure from powerful outside constituencies.

We have a long way to go to meet these two criteria. There is a crisis in our political culture, with half the potential voting population not even bothering to take part in the rituals of democracy such as voting and communicating with elected representatives. There are indications that voter disenfranchisement is a frightening reality, as we saw in the last two presidential elections (in Florida in 2000 and Ohio in 2004). Several organizations have filed lawsuits questioning the legality of the 2004 election results in Ohio, claiming that, some Ohio voters were given false information about voting times, were forced to wait in lines for hours, and in some cases were harassed. A congressional inquiry released in January of 2005 by democrats on the House Judiciary Committee found "numerous, serious election irregularities in the Ohio presidential election, which resulted in a

significant disenfranchisement of voters. Cumulatively, these irregularities, which affected hundreds of thousands of votes and voters in
Ohio, raise grave doubts regarding whether it can be said the Ohio
electors selected on December 13, 2004, were chosen in a manner
that conforms to Ohio law, let alone federal requirements and constitutional standards."[5]

The many pressures on this congressional system as it works to
prepare the budget each year also compromise democracy. Pressure
itself is not a bad thing — elected representatives need to hear the
views of their constituents and understand the issues they face.
However, the power of business and corporate interests to be heard
and to buy influence with their contributions far outweighs the ability of regular citizens and most nonprofit organizations to influence
the process.

One particular pressure that hangs over members of Congress and
the president is the unrelenting stress of raising the money they need
to win election or re-election. A look at the amount of money incumbents attract tells the story. In the 2004 election cycle, incumbents in
the Senate raised an average of $8.6 million, with challengers collect-
ing an average of $969,000. In the House, incumbents raised an aver-
age of $1.1 million; challengers, an average of $192,000. Those who
do get elected to Congress tend to stay there — in 2004, incumbents
in the House had a 98 percent re-election rate, while those in the senate had an 85 percent rate. (Comprehensive information on money
in politics is available from the Center for Responsive Politics <www.
opensecert.org>, which is where much of the information in this section came from.)

Of the billions spent each election cycle, most is donated in checks
exceeding $1,000, but less than 1/10 of one percent of the general
population make individual contributions at this rate. This means
that extremely wealthy individuals and corporations are making most
of the contributions, which gives them a disproportionate influence
on the politicians. You can tell who the powerful members of Congress
are by the size of donations they receive from political action committees (PACs) and individuals. Among group contributions, more
than 90 percent come from corporations.

Raising this money not only takes an enormous amount of energy
that would be better spent making the momentous decisions required

of a senator or representative, but it also leaves members of Congress vulnerable to the influence of corporate lobbyists and agendas. For instance, members of the House Financial Services Committee — formerly known as the Banking Committee — which has jurisdiction over policy related to banks, savings and loan institutions, insurance, and securities — received $10 million from the banks, finance, and insurance, PACs in the 2004 election.

The huge amounts of money needed to finance a run for Congress have produced a bizarre yet predictable situation. In 2002, almost 43 percent of the incoming freshmen members of Congress — 27 lawmakers — were millionaires, even though millionaires make up only one percent of the American population. The Senate is now so full of wealthy people that it has been dubbed the Millionaires' Club. At least 40 out of the 100 senators are millionaires, and many are multimillionaires. We know this because each member must file a financial disclosure form. However, these forms can be vague, and they do not include information on the pensions and salaries members of Congress receive, so there are probably many more millionaires in the group. The three wealthiest senators as of 2003 were Democrats: John Kerry of Massachusetts, with a net worth of at least $164 million; Herb Kohl of Wisconsin, with a net worth of at least $111 million; and John "Jay" Rockefeller of West Virginia, with a net worth of at least $82 million.[6]

Many members of Congress are not only extremely wealthy, but they also sit on the boards of, own stock in, and/or have influence with companies that have a large stake in the proceedings of Congress. Two prominent examples are the pharmaceutical and oil industries. This interconnection is obviously a factor as the House and Senate deliberate on issues such as the Medicare drug benefit, and drilling for oil in the Alaskan wilderness.

Who Benefits? The Power Elite

As PIs, we may notice that the people sitting in the House and the Senate are not representative of the population. This is another indication that the system is not functioning in a truly democratic way. Besides being unfair in terms of excluding people from taking part in decisions, it also means that the voices of those most negatively affected by key budget decisions are not heard.

The first thing we notice is that women are severely underrepresented. They constitute 51.3 percent of the population, but only 13.8 percent of the Congress (13.7 percent of the House and 14 percent of the Senate). This would be striking enough on its own, but when compared to women's representation in other national parliaments, it is astounding.

According to the Interparliamentary Union in Geneva, Switzerland, the United States ranks 59th in the world in terms of the percentage of women in its national legislative bodies. The top five countries — all with women making up over 35 percent of their legislatures — are Rwanda, Sweden, Denmark, Finland, and the Netherlands. Rwanda and Sweden have over 45 percent representation by women, and there are more than 16 countries that have 30 percent or more. Countries that have a higher percentage than the United States include: the United Kingdom, Trinidad and Tobago, Mexico, Vietnam, South Africa, and Bulgaria. Women in the United States were only granted the right to vote in 1920 after a bitter struggle, and clearly there is a long way to go to insure full participation of women in governing the nation.

According to the 2000 census, the population of the United States is 69.1 percent white; 12.1 percent African American; 12.5 percent Hispanic; 3.7 percent Asian or Pacific Islander; 0.7 percent American Indian; and 0.2 percent some other race. Just over 1.5 percent indicated that their heritage included two or more races.

However, here is the makeup of the Congress: 86.7 percent white; 7.2 percent African American; 4.6 percent Hispanic; 0.93 percent

PI POINTER

Research on men and women legislators carried out in Britain in 1996 showed that although both women and men viewed economic issues as a priority, women were more concerned about part-time work, low pay, and pension rights, while men were more concerned about unemployment.[7]

Asian or Pacific Islander; and 0.56 percent American Indian. As of 2000 there were no Hispanics, African Americans, or Asian or Pacific Islanders in the Senate.

One of the main reasons our political system is not yet fully democratic is that a small elite of the upper class dominates the economy and politics. According to G. William Domhoff, a leading theoretician studying class influence in politics, the upper class makes up about 0.5 percent of the population and generally consists of those people who attend particular schools, join certain clubs, and participate in common social activities. The members of the upper class own 20 to 25 percent of all privately held wealth and 45 to 50 percent of all privately held corporate stock.

Domhoff calls this group "relatively fixed," meaning that although there is some change, essentially it continues functioning in the same way over time. He defines the power elite as a small group of Americans who own and manage large banks and corporations, finance the political campaigns of conservative Democrats and virtually all Republicans at the state and national levels, and serve in government as appointed officials and military leaders. We can see from the statistics above that although some women and people of color have been allowed to join, white males of the upper class still dominate the economy and government.

The power elite retains its control of the federal government through a variety of organizations and methods including an interlocking set of policy discussion groups, foundations, think tanks, and university institutions. These provide social cohesion and a common economic outlook, and have a huge impact on social policy, even if popular opinion differs from the views of the corporate elite. Also, because our society puts high value on privately owned property and individual wealth, those who run the power structure will reflect those values in the public policy they create. In a book he wrote with Richard L. Zemiegenhoff, *Diversity in the Power Elite,* Domhoff pointed out that "those who have more of what is valued have more power."

Another reason the political power elite stays relatively fixed is the structure of the US electoral system. The winner-take-all system is one of the major challenges women and people of color face when they try to gain representation in the political system that is in proportion to their representation in the population. There is a range of proposals for changing voting systems and encouraging higher voter participation. These include proportional representation or instant run-off elections, and all are combined with true campaign finance reform. These strategies could change the lock the two parties now have on the system and would go a long way to finally achieving the democracy we say we value in the United States. More democracy, in turn, would lead to better debate, and decisions, about what should be funded by the national budget.

PART 2

❖

Connecting the Dots

I N PART ONE WE LOOKED AT the basics of the budget as public investi-gators (PIs) and uncovered many of the hidden realities of income, expenses, debt, surplus, and the budget process. Now in Part Two we will examine two aspects of the larger context of the budget: in Chapter 6 we will look at how the budget interacts with the economy in the United States, and in Chapter 7, how the US budget interacts with the global economy.

CHAPTER 6

❖

The Budget and the US Economy

T HE FEDERAL BUDGET DOES NOT EXIST IN A VACUUM. It is part of a value system, a worldview, and a set of relationships that are known as "the economy." News reports about the economy often use jargon and complex analyses that can make the rest of us feel we don't really understand it. Yet understanding the economy is as simple as really noticing what is going on around you.

As you look at your community or city, these are some of the things you might notice: some people have lots more income and wealth than they require to meet their basic needs; some have enough income and wealth to meet their basic needs; and some do not have enough income and wealth to meet their basic needs. You will see that most people work for pay for a company or organization, but their relationships with their employers vary widely. Some workers have high pay and benefits from their jobs, some have low pay and no benefits, and some are not able to work or cannot find work. You will notice that banks, government, and large companies have a lot of influence on how things evolve in your community. People who own property, especially in more expensive neighborhoods, often have more say about the quality of the schools and community infrastructure in their neighborhoods than people who don't own property — and the result is that schools and infrastructure in wealthy neighborhoods are often better and better funded than is the case in lower-income neighborhoods.

As you look around, you will also notice how race, class, and gender interact within the economy. When I was growing up in Washington, DC, I remember taking the bus to public junior high school from an upper-middle-class neighborhood. Our bus was filled with students and with professionals, mostly white, going to work from our neighborhood to various government agencies downtown. As we passed buses going the other way, we saw they were filled with African American women on their way to clean the houses of the professionals on our bus. This was my introduction to the economy in a city that was officially non-segregated but was, in fact, segregated by race, class, and gender.

Capitalism in the United States

The economic system we live under is called capitalism. It came into being during the 16th century as a result of historical, social, geographic, and other factors as Europe, particularly England, began to dominate economic relations around the world. Capitalism is based on the premise that capital (land, buildings, machines, other equipment, and wealth in the form of stocks, bonds, and bank accounts) is privately owned, and that economic activity involves the interaction of buyers and sellers (or producers), organized in markets. The key point that PIs need to recognize is that, under capitalism, the owners of land and capital have the freedom to pursue profit using their resources and the labor of workers.

As we saw when we looked around our communities, different people have different relationships to this economic system: some are owners with a lot of wealth and income; some are managers with an excess of wealth and income; some are workers who may or may not have enough wealth and income; and some are poor and unemployed, with few economic resources.

Capitalism has evolved since it came into being and is still evolving. Capitalism in the United States in the early 21st century is characterized by the dominance of large multinational corporations, some of which have incomes larger than many countries. The law gives these corporations protection to pursue these profits without regard to human or environmental impacts, and economists still tell us today that allowing the market to be "free" — to operate without any governmental restrictions on the interactions between producers and consumers — will result in the greatest good for all. They imply that government has no role to play in regulating these interactions or protecting consumers, but in reality there never has been a free market. Government has always subsidized corporations, as we saw in Chapter 1.

There are a few things we need to keep in mind about how our economic system evolved. Corporations did not always enjoy the legal protection they have today, nor did they always have the privilege to pursue profit at the expense of workers, communities, and the environment. In the early years of our country's history, states had the authority to charter corporations, and for a hundred years after the signing of the Constitution, citizen vigilance and activism forced legislators to keep corporations on a short leash. Because of widespread opposition to corporations, early state legislators granted few charters. They denied charters altogether when communities opposed the plans of prospective corporations. Citizens governed corporations by specifying rules and operating conditions, not just in corporate charters, but also in state constitutions and laws.

However, some corporations still managed to become large and powerful. Because the national government was small in the 19th century — partly due to the great power invested in the states — there were powerful corporations before there was a large national government. This meant that those who ran the corporations had a lot of input into the direction the national government took when it began to grow, and they made sure one of its major focuses was to uphold the right to private property, and to provide law and order, so that capitalism could function freely.

The Program on Corporations, Law and Democracy (www.poclad. org) provides some history of the laws that helped corporations gain power as the country evolved. POCLAD's research shows that the biggest blow to citizen control of our democracy came in 1886, when the US Supreme Court ruled in *Santa Clara County v. Southern Pacific Railroad* that a private corporation was a "natural person" under the US Constitution, sheltered by the 14th Amendment, which requires due process in the criminal prosecution of "persons." Following this ruling, huge and wealthy corporations were allowed to compete on equal terms with neighborhood businesses and individuals. Sixty years later, Supreme Court justice William O. Douglas wrote: "There was no history, logic, or reason given to support that view."[1]

It was not until the 1930s, during the Great Depression, that the federal government began to intervene in the capitalist economy on

PI POINTER

The Supreme Court declared corporations "natural persons," protected under the Constitution, years before women could even vote.

behalf of workers. Under the New Deal administration of President Franklin Roosevelt, the government introduced Social Security and Unemployment Insurance to provide a minimum of protection to workers and their families. The debate about how much the government should intervene in the economy on behalf of the general well-being of the people of the United States is still very much alive in the early 21st century.

US capitalism also grew hand in hand with a strong military and international intervention that enhanced the country's economic position globally. In the 19th century the US military intervened in several countries in Latin America and Asia. The national government was greatly expanded during World War I and World War II in order to coordinate the country's participation in the wars and to secure global influence afterwards. After World War II, the military establishment stayed large as it maintained military bases and engaged in military actions around the world. Ever since then, military spending has been a large portion of discretionary budget expenses (as discussed in Chapter 2), with the amount spiking during wars.

These two aspects of capitalism in the United States — government support of corporations and a large military — are interwoven because the recipients of most military spending are big corporations that make weapons. This has had a huge impact on how the national budget evolved. Since World War II, trillions of dollars have gone to the military, and defense contractors have made huge profits from taxpayers' money. As we have seen in previous chapters, there are tax breaks and subsidies for corporations on both the income and expense sides of the budget, and these have been knit into the very fabric of the budget. The national government and giant corporations have developed together.

How these priorities affect the national budget and our commitments as a country was brought home to me many times when I worked in Washington as a lobbyist for peace and women's organizations. All too frequently, funding for programs that made a difference in people's lives, particularly the lives of low-income women and their children, were cut or limited while military spending increased. When the military was cut back, it was often at the expense of benefits or equipment for soldiers on the ground.

During preparation for the Gulf War in 1990, Congress voted an increase in military spending to cover the costs of the war. I was executive director of the Women's International League for Peace and Freedom at the time, and I was mystified by this increase because it came on top of huge annual military spending that was supposed to prepare the Department of Defense to fight wars. At the same time, the Department of Agriculture announced a cutback in the number of people who would be served by the Women's Infants and Children program (WIC), which provides crucial nutritional support and information to low-income mothers and their infants. The program was cut back because the price of milk had increased. Instead of increasing the funding for the program to pay for the milk, WIC was forced to absorb the milk price increase at the expense of mothers and children.

Billions of dollars of US taxpayers' money is being spent in Iraq when millions of people here at home have no health insurance and inadequate food and housing. Most of the money set aside to help Iraq will end up going to private contractors — corporations — who get government contracts to rebuild Iraq's roads, retrain its police force, operate its airports, service US troops, and make a profit. The most prominent of these corporations is Halliburton, which is making huge profits from its work in Iraq and which received contracts without going through a competitive bidding process. The government/military/corporate connections insure that taxpayers heavily subsidize corporations.

According to writer William Greider, capitalism has had another effect on the United States in this phase of history. "National governments have lost ground on the whole, partly because many have retreated from trying to exercise their power over commerce and finance. In advanced economies most governments have become mere sales-men, promoting the fortunes of their own multi-nationals. Evidence it's not working for all people is the condition of labor markets — either mass unemployment or declining real wages."[2] In the US we have had both high unemployment and declining wages for years, while many US multinational corporations, including banks and mutual fund companies, have made huge profits playing in the global economy.

PI POINTER

The Women's Infants and Children's Program (WIC) ensures mothers are healthy, gives infants and children a good foundation, and saves money on future health care. Yet there is not enough money currently in the budget to support all who are eligible. We could fund all the women and infants who need the program for the cost of a few Abrams tanks.

The Federal Budget and Economic Equity

Although economic equity is not the focus of the federal budget, the budget can be, and in the past has been, used to lessen economic inequality. In fact, the idea of consciously using the budget to enact economic policy promoting equality has been the focus of a major debate in economics. John Maynard Keynes, a prominent economist in the first half of the 20th century, advocated that the government use its money to achieve full employment, even if it created a deficit. Full employment would be a boon to the economy, according to Keynes, and the fact that employed people would pay taxes and buy goods and services made it well worth the investment. He also argued against cutting wages, saying that the decrease in workers' buying power would hurt the economy.

Social Security was enacted in 1935 to insure that elderly Americans did not live in dire poverty and that a pension was guaranteed for working Americans. The Social Security Act also mandated the provision of disability and survivors' benefits. After World War II, the government created grants to allow returning GIs to buy homes, and it created safety nets in the form of welfare, unemployment compensation, and public service jobs that helped to ensure people would still be able to purchase goods and services when the economy hit a downward cycle. These programs provided a minimum of protection to single mothers and recently unemployed workers. If the programs were often inadequate and didn't reach all who were eligible, at least they kept many people from having to live in complete economic crisis. Medicare, Medicaid, and tax credits for low-income working people (such as the Earned Income Tax Credit, described in Chapter 2) are examples of more recent programs that have been created to provide a safety net for people when the economy alone does not.

PI POINTER

The combined wealth of the top 5 percent of American families is more than the wealth of the remaining 95 percent of the population, collectively. This is the highest wealth inequality of any industrialized country, and the greatest wealth gap in the US since 1929.

The budget is also used to increase class inequality. In the last 20 years, many of these safety net programs have been cut, and tax policies have been revised to benefit the wealthy and corporations at the expense of people at the bottom of the economic ladder. These national policy decisions have contributed to the increasing gap between the haves and the have-nots in America. Since the 1970s, the top one percent of households have doubled their share of the national wealth.

In the last 25 years labor unions have been under attack, and many have been broken, which leads to a reduction in the number of jobs that pay well and provide good benefits. The federal minimum wage has been held at $5.15, welfare and housing programs have been cut, and many government services have been taken out of the public sector and put into the hand of private corporations. As mentioned in Chapter 1, when government services are privatized and government spending reduced, many women and people of color lose good public sector jobs that pay higher wages than other jobs they would otherwise have access to.

The Federal Budget and the States

The federal government has always been economically intertwined with the states. Originally, states were given land and received aid to help with natural disasters and security issues. The grants-in-aid system began to take shape in the early 20th century, when the government required matching funding from the states for some programs and began to set conditions for receiving grants. This grants-in-aid system was used extensively to implement policy during the Great Depression and the New Deal era, while the Great Society programs of the 1960s invested in urban areas and provided assistance for poor and low-income people.

The Nixon administration implemented a program of block grants and revenue sharing, which gave the states money with no conditions on how they spent it. In recent decades, some of the big federal programs, such as Medicaid, food stamps, and Section 8 subsidized housing, have been set up as joint federal/state programs. This means that both levels of government contribute funding, and the state has to meet certain conditions to receive the federal money.

If the program is set up as an entitlement, then all eligible people who are registered will receive the service, no matter how much it costs. Many programs, including welfare (now known as Temporary Assistance to Needy Families), have been converted from entitlements to block grants. Block grants give the states more leeway to decide how to spend the money, and when the money runs out, eligible people can lose the service. Because many states have faced fiscal crises in recent years, they have been forced to cut money from valuable programs. Partly this is due to the fact that most states are required by law to balance their books, so they cannot run a deficit in order to invest in programs or services when the economy is in recession. If states do not maintain contingency funds for times of high unemployment (when fewer people are paying taxes and more people are using government programs), and if they are not willing to raise taxes, they may find they cannot maintain much-needed social programs, and will end up cutting them. In addition, states are subject to the shifting relationship with the federal government — different administrations have different views of federal/state/local relationships — and this may affect the funding they receive from Washington.

In the first years of the new millennium, many states have been reeling from dire fiscal crises, and the federal government has not been coming forward to help. Budget shortfalls have caused some states to reduce the numbers of teachers or firefighters they employ, stop buying textbooks, cut or stop after-school programs, release prisoners early, and cut police protection at a time when we are supposed to be focusing on "homeland security." According to OMB Watch, in 2003 almost every state cut Medicaid eligibility, thereby endangering the health of children, poor adults, pregnant women, and disabled people.

Medicaid is one of the states' largest expenditures, coming right after education. President Bush proposed cutting $60 billion from Medicaid in his fiscal 2006 budget proposal. This kind of federal policy will further stress state budgets and will force them to cut benefits. Women are the vast majority of recipients of Medicaid, either as single heads of households or in nursing homes. The Bush administration has also floated proposals for ending Medcaid's status as an entitlement and converting it to a block grant. This would be a disaster for millions of low-income Americans, as Medicaid is the only guaranteed health insurer for people who do not have the money to pay for health insurance or who are not covered through their employment.

Federal Reserve System

It is impossible to understand the US economy without understanding the Federal Reserve system and how it functions. Congress established the Federal Reserve — or the "Fed" as it is known — when it passed the Federal Reserve Act of 1913. The Fed was intended to create a stable banking system for the country. It was a response to the upheaval caused by bank crises and monetary collapses during the late 1800s and early 1900s. The act created a central banking system divided into regional Federal Reserve banks.

The Banking Act of 1935 and the Monetary Control Act of 1980 added provisions and responsibilities to the Fed's original mandate. The Banking Act of 1935, coming on the heels of the Great Depression, gave the leadership of the Fed to a centralized board of governors, appointed by the president and approved by the Senate. The Monetary Control Act of 1980 made some further changes in the system, including giving the Fed authority to charge a fee for services it provided to member banks.

So what is the Fed? It is a bank that issues the national currency, exerts control over the direction and extent of changes in the national money supply, plays a major role in the supervision and regulation of banks, and is the bank for the federal government and the banking community. The Fed is similar to what is known as the "central bank" of other major industrialized capitalist countries.

A board of governors — a group of bankers appointed by the president for 14-year terms — controls the Fed from its base in Washington, DC. The president appoints one member of the board to serve as Fed chairman for a four-year term. Those terms can be renewed (for example, Alan Greenspan has been Fed chairman since 1987). The majority of the Fed's day-to-day operations are in the hands of the officers of 12 district Federal Reserve banks, located throughout the nation. Most commercial banks are members of the Fed, and those that are members of the Fed own stock in these Federal Reserve banks.

The reason this central bank is called the Federal Reserve is because all banks are required to put a percentage of their deposits — the money people and businesses put into the banks — in reserve with the Fed. The banks are then allowed to lend and invest the rest of their funds, paying depositors interest for the use of their money. The percentage of this "reserve requirement" changes, but is currently approximately 10 percent. The purpose of the reserve requirement is to make sure banks do not lend out or invest all their deposits, which could lead to bank failure and insecurity among depositors.

One of the Fed's major responsibilities is to decide on monetary policy, which means it decides how much money will be in circulation at any given time. The Fed can affect the flow of money in several ways. First, it can change the reserve requirement for banks, allowing them to lend or invest more or less money. Second, the Fed can change interest rates on the money it lends, which affects all interest rates offered by banks and financial institutions. However, the main way the Fed influences the supply of money is through open market operations, which are small adjustments conducted several times a week. The Fed is allowed to buy or sell US government bonds, which changes the supply of reserves and the circulation of money throughout the system. The Fed buys bonds when it wants to lower interest rates, and sells bonds when it wants to raise interest rates.

The Fed is sometimes referred to as the fourth branch of government because its actions can have such a profound impact on the economy. Yet it is not subject to the checks and balances and accountability that the other branches of government are. The board of governors is formally independent of the executive branch and protected by tenure. And although the Fed was created by Congress and is dependent upon it for its continued existence, it is self-financing and so is not subject to scrutiny under the budget process.

The Fed tends to be shielded from public attention because most people know little about it. Politicians who have tried to address the extraordinary power of the Fed find it difficult to get attention from the media and the public, and as a result, they rarely achieve concrete results. For instance, Representative Wright Patman (D-TX), former chair of the House Banking Committee and a member of Congress from 1929 to 1976, made change in the Fed his major priority. He and others after him introduced legislation each year to make the Fed more democratic and less subject to the influence of major banks. Yet no Fed reform legislation has ever succeeded. Patman observed:

> There should be no mystery whatsoever — no secrecy
> — concerning the control of money supply, interest
> rates, or credit ... These are matters affecting the public
> from the time they get up in the morning until they
> retire at night. For the Federal Reserve and the banker-
> oriented Open Market Committee to cloak the working
> of the money system in a mantle of secrecy is to violate
> the prime rule of a free society ... The Constitution
> wisely provides that Congress shall coin money and
> regulate its value ... If monetary matters are left to the

Federal Reserve, insulated from the people, then the public will have no way to express its approval or disapproval of their actions. The fact is an independent Federal Reserve means something that is not in the framework of our constitutional system, which says that Congress will make the laws and the President shall execute them. Those who desire a dictatorship on money matters by a "bankers club" — away from the Congress and the President — are in effect advocating another form of government alien to our own.[3]

Other than being concerned about the Fed's undemocratic nature, why should we care about monetary policy and the role of the Fed in our nation's past, present, and future? In recent decades the Fed has had as a primary goal of keeping inflation down. If there is too much money in circulation, inflation — a general increase in prices — can be a result. At a certain point this can cause sales to lag and corporate profits to slow. Before that point is reached, the Fed might increase interest rates so it is harder for people to get credit. This generally decreases the amount of money available. This is called a "tight money" policy, and because it makes it harder for businesses to get credit, it can lead to wage cuts and layoffs. The effect of a tight money policy is often an increase in unemployment, and higher unemployment is seen as a necessary sacrifice to make it possible to "wring inflation from the economy."

One of the problems with this approach to dealing with inflation is that inflation, if it is not too extreme, actually improves the financial situation of huge numbers of working-class and middle-class people. Those who own their own homes and are dependent on their wages for income benefit from stable or increasing wages. The opposite of tight money is easy money — in other words, low interest rates that make credit cheaper and easier for people to borrow.

People with fixed financial assets — for example, investments and huge savings — rely on high interest rates to give them a bigger return on their investments. So the Fed, with its tight money policy, can be seen as protecting banks, other creditors, and wealthy people who benefit from high interest rates. Legally, the Fed has the power to decide how high interest rates will be. Keeping them high is a big advantage to those who are primarily creditors, but it is a disadvantage to those who are primarily debtors, which is the majority of people. According to the Fed's own figures, more than half of American households are net debtors.

The Full Employment and Balanced Growth Act of 1978 (known as the Humphrey-Hawkins Act) was an effort by Senator Hubert Humphrey (D-MN) and others to focus government policy on the suffering of jobless workers. One provision of the bill gives the Fed a mandate — in other words, it is required by law — to include full employment in its goals as it implements monetary policy. Under the Humphrey-Hawkins Act, the Fed chairman is required to come before the House and Senate banking committees twice a year to explain the Fed's monetary goals and to demonstrate how achieving these goals will affect employment.

PI POINTER

Although the Fed is required by law to view return on investment and full employment as equal goals, Fed monetary policy consistently puts return on investment ahead of full employment.

In recent years the definition of "full employment" has changed, with 4 or 5 percent unemployment considered close enough to full. As of 2004, the unemployment rate is 5.4 percent, which means that, according to the Fed, there is full employment. One of the problems with this definition, though, is how the numbers are measured. Official government statistics measure only those people who are looking for full-time work. This leaves out those who have stopped looking for work or who work in part-time or contingent jobs but would prefer full-time jobs with benefits. The Fed actually came up with a new measure — the Augmented Unemployment Rate — that includes the discouraged and the underemployed. In 1999 the Fed began to include this augmented unemployment rate in its Humphrey-Hawkins report. Currently, the augmented unemployment rate is 9 percent. The real unemployment rate is probably much higher.

What the Fed does has a profound impact on the federal budget. Remember the discussion of the national debt in Chapter 4? When interest rates go up or down a few percentage points, it translates into billions of dollars lost or gained by those who lent the money to the government. It also means billions of dollars more or less that the government has to pay in interest. And if the Fed's actions cause unemployment to rise, the federal budget must increase its social welfare payments to cover unemployment and other assistance.

GDP and Unpaid Work

As modern capitalism and the field of economics have evolved, new ways to measure the economy and new terms to describe it have also emerged. These terms may intimidate or confuse us, but they have also come to influence the way we think about ourselves and our relations with others in our country and with other countries.

It is important to keep in mind that this is only one way of describing the world, and as we will see, it is not the most accurate or inclusive way. If we can see and describe the world differently, we can create a different reality.

One of the terms that we hear over and over is GDP, which stands for gross domestic product. This is a measure of the value of the total amount of goods and services produced within the country over a specified time, normally a year. It is used to measure the productivity of the economy. The GDP is calculated by adding personal spending, government spending, investment, and net exports (exports minus imports). In 2004 the United States GDP was $10.9 trillion.

Included in the calculation of GDP are consumer goods (things that households buy) and investment goods (things such as machines, office buildings, and bridges). These are two kinds of output, and the GDP adds these two basic kinds of output together, along with public sector or government purchases and investments (i.e., teacher services and roads). The GDP gives us a large view of the economy, what economists call macroeconomics. This view lets us see patterns in the economy, such as unemployment, inflation, and growth.

Microeconomics shows us the effect individual buying, saving, and investment decisions have on the economy.

You may have also seen references to GNP, which stands for gross national product. GNP is a measure of the goods and services produced by the residents of a country, regardless of where the assets are located. It includes income from US investments aboard. Although GNP is often measured, GDP is the figure usually used internationally to compare the economies of countries. GDP measures only moneymaking activities. The goods and services that are exchanged in the market for money are considered productive. It defines what businesses produce as wealth, and it defines a "good" economy as one that has a rising GDP.

One important thing to know about the GDP is that it is the "official" figure used to compare the productivity of different countries. In order to compile the GDP figure, each country uses a formula called the System of National Accounts (SNA), which has been accepted by most nations and is the international standard used by the United Nations (UN), the Commission of the European Communities, the International Monetary Fund, the Organization for Economic Co-operation and Development, and the World Bank to do international comparisons.

The SNA reflects a particular value system that has profoundly affected how we all see the world. The methodology that underlies it was developed by an assistant to economist John Maynard Keynes when Keynes was charged with providing the British government with a detailed analysis of the nation's wartime economy. So the framework was created during World War II, when what was considered most valuable was items produced for use in the war. These national accounts have therefore institutionalized the value of military production and preparation. As we saw in Chapter 3, this influence is visible in the way government itemizes non-mandatory expenses, which are divided into "defense" and "nondefense." When the SNA was put in place, the United States stopped officially calculating national wealth and used this more narrow measure of worth and value.

As Marilyn Waring points out in her book *Counting for Nothing*, huge chunks of reality are left out of the national accounts and so, in effect, "don't count." Some of the parts left out include the Earth, the environment, unpaid labor (most of which is performed by women), and all sorts of activities that women (and many men) consider to be productive. Because these are not included in the official measure, they are devalued, and the result is a bizarre accounting. The GDP may be going up, thus indicating growth and an improving economy, while forests are being destroyed, high-wage jobs are disappearing, and government services to communities are being cut back. The idea that growth itself is good, separated from the context of what is actually happening in the real world, is absurd.

PI POINTER

The value of housework in the US is estimated at $1.4 billion a year. The unpaid and officially uncounted contributions of women to the economy are a massive subsidy. When government services are cut back, it is assumed that women will do more in their communities and homes to make up for the loss of public support.

Although women have different roles and status depending on age, class, race, and other factors, most women make major contributions to the national wealth — other than as workers and taxpayers — that go unrecognized or for which they do not receive monetary compensation. Women's childbearing, childrearing, care of the family (which often includes elderly parents in addition to children), household chores, and volunteer work in the community provide the foundation for economic productivity, but are not valued in the official statistics. According to the UN Development Program, the value of women's unwaged work worldwide is estimated at $11 trillion.

A study by Britain's Office for National Statistics focused on the amount of unpaid work that takes place in the British economy. According to the study, GDP would have been between 44 and 104 percent higher if unpaid work such as babysitting, childcare, and household maintenance were included. (Although women do not do all that work, they do most of it.) The study also found that the average adult spends almost twice as much time each day performing unpaid work as he or she does doing paid work. Activities the study defined as unpaid work included gardening, looking after children, volunteer work, and transportation, such as bringing children to school. Similar time-use studies are now being done in many countries, thanks to organizing by women around the globe, and the data they produce will be included in what are called satellite accounts in the official national accounts. The US government conducted its first time-use study in 2003.

Many economists now call this realm of uncounted and uncompensated labor the care economy. Economist Diane Elson describes it this way:

> The care economy produces family and community-oriented goods and services as part of the process of caring for people. Work in the care economy is not paid, though it may be supported by transfer payments from the government (such as pensions and child benefits). It is regulated by social norms rather than by commercial or bureaucratic criteria. This economy is excluded, as a matter of principle, from the UN System of National Accounts. Both men and women work in the care economy, but overall it is relatively intensive in the use of female labour. The care economy contributes to the welfare of the individuals receiving care, but it also contributes to the activities of the commodity economy and the public service economy by supplying human resources and by maintaining the social framework (supplying what some economists call human capital and social capital to the commodity economy and public service economy). [emphasis in original]

Public policy does not take into account what women need in order to be able to perform these tasks when public support is cut back or eliminated. If the full breadth of women's contribution to the productivity of the economy were counted, we would need a different measure than the GDP or SNA to reflect it.

It is important for women to understand that what are called "transfer payments" (in other words, the support for families and elderly people provided by social programs like housing assistance, which are funded by national resources in the budget) are also not included in the GDP. Within the official framework, "transfer payments" for military contractors building weapons systems are productive. Investments in individuals and families that enable people to live better lives and participate more fully in the economy and in their communities are not productive.

If women's main contributions to the economy and the national community are invisible in the official economic measures, women are denied recognition and compensation for their contributions, but they also lose the chance to have greater visibility, power, and influence in the larger social/economic arena. The lack of visibility, recognition, and compensation is internalized and, along with other internalized messages from a male-dominated society, keeps women silent and without the financial independence that would enable them to take action on their own behalf and on behalf of their families and communities.

One example of how women's lack of visibility and power denies them financial independence is the absence of pay equity in the economy. Equal pay has been enshrined in law since 1963, but today, 38 years later, women are still paid less than men — even when they have similar education, skills, and experience. Women are paid 75 cents for every dollar men receive That's $25 less to spend on groceries, housing, childcare, and other expenses for every $100 worth of work they do. Over a lifetime of work, the 25 cents on the dollar that women are losing adds up. Working families in the US lose $200

PI POINTER

According to the Coalition of Labor Union Women, the average 25-year-old working woman will lose more than $523,000 to unequal pay during her working life.

billion of income annually to the wage gap. If the pay equity law were enforced, women in the labor force would be able to support their families and would move towards financial independence.

Alternatives to the GDP

Many organizations have been working to create alternatives to the GDP that can be used to measure productivity, development, and value. One that is now widely used internationally is the Human Development Index (HDI) of the UN Development Program. The HDI is a summary composite index that measures a country's average achievements in three basic aspects of human development:

❖ Longevity, which is measured by life expectancy at birth

❖ Knowledge, which is measured by a combination of the adult literacy rate and the combined primary, secondary, and tertiary gross enrollment ratio

❖ Standard of living, which is measured by GDP per capita.

The United States is first in the world if GDP is used as a measure, but the HDI looks at how that wealth is used within the country. The United States ranks 6th in the world on the HDI, and when that index is adjusted for indicators of poverty (the HDI 2) the United States is ranked 17th in the world.

On the Gender-related Development Index (GDI), which adjusts for inequality between men and women, the US ranks 4th. The GDI is a composite indicator that measures the a country's average achievement in the same three areas as the HDI, but it also considers gender inequalities. The Gender Empowerment Measure (GEM) measures whether women and men are equally able to participate in economic and political life. On this scale, the United States ranks 10th.

Another international indicator is the Environmental Sustainability Index (ESI), which is a measure of overall progress towards environmental sustainability in 142 countries. The United States ranks 45th. ESI scores are based on a set of 20 core "indicators." This permits cross-national comparisons of environmental progress in a systematic and quantitative fashion. It represents a first step to a more analytical approach to environmental decision making. The ESI is the result of collaboration among the World Economic Forum's Global Leaders for Tomorrow Environment Task Force, the Yale

Center for Environmental Law and Policy, and the Columbia University Center for International Earth Science Information Network.

The Total Economy

Another way to get a perspective on what we are taught about the economy is to put it in a larger context. The "official" economy (as measured by the GDP) is only one part of a full picture of productive activity and resources in our society.

The GDP includes the production of goods and services that are sold in order to make money. As pointed out in this chapter, the following items are some of the things left out of this official economic measure:

❖ The resources of the Earth

❖ Unpaid labor (mostly supplied by women)

❖ Volunteer and community work

❖ The informal cash economy.

Figure 6.1 shows the multifaceted nature of the full economic picture. It starts from the bottom (#1) and goes up.

The earth and ecosystem are the foundation for all the economy's productivity. They provide the resources on which everything else rests.

The next level of the foundation is labor, paid and unpaid. This includes all the home, family, and community work that is performed mostly by women, the whole care economy.

The "official" economy (on which the GDP is based) is made up of the two top levels, the public and private sector and the formal cash economy. The private sector is considered the most valuable part of the official economy, and the other levels serve it.

In an alternative framework, one that respected and valued all productive resources and activities, all levels would be valued, and the private sector would be grounded in the others.

The Total Economy

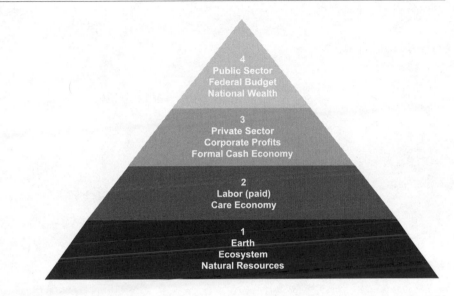

figure 6.1

CHAPTER 7

❖

The Budget and
the Global Economy

THE US BUDGET IS SO VAST, and the economic, military, and political position of the United States in the world is so central, that the US national budget actually affects everyone in the world. Some of these effects are direct and funded through expenses in the budget — for example, military interventions or foreign aid programs — and some are written into the tax code, such as tax breaks for US corporate operations that encourage exploitative labor practices in other countries. Although the budget is a tool that creates, funds, and maintains programs and policies that have a profound effect on others in the world, most Americans are unaware that these things are included in the budget or funded by tax money.

In this chapter we will examine some of the components of the budget that affect the global economy. Then we'll take a look at some of the efforts in countries around the world to create national budgets responsive to issues surrounding gender, poverty, and the environment.

Financial Institutions

In order to understand the interaction between the US budget and the global economy, we need to travel back to 1944, near the end of World War II. In July of that year, representatives of 44 industrialized countries gathered at Bretton Woods, a resort in New Hampshire, to create structures for managing the world economy in the aftermath of the war's destruction. The participants at this Bretton Woods Conference set up an international monetary system, adopting the US dollar as the world's currency for two reasons: most countries defined their own currencies in terms of the dollar; and the United States held most of the world's gold supply, which was used as the exchange commodity. The participants at the conference also created two institutions: the International Monetary Fund (IMF) and the International Bank for Reconstruction and Development, now known as the World Bank.

The IMF was set up to promote international monetary cooperation and facilitate the growth of international trade. The fund's resources were to be made available to all countries. The World Bank was designed to facilitate investment in countries and to provide loans to members for development projects. Originally most of the World Bank's loans went to the European countries rebuilding after the war. Since the 1960s, however, most of the bank's loans have gone to developing countries in Africa, Asia, and Latin America. The World Bank and the IMF have emerged as central institutions in the global economy, and, along with the World Trade Organization (WTO), they dominate economic relations between the North and the South.

The programs and policies of these institutions have been harmful to many people in the world. When they were created, their mandate was to help prevent future conflicts by lending money for reconstruction and development and by smoothing out temporary problems in the balance of payments. ("Balance of payments" refers to the relationship between the amount of money a nation spends abroad and the income it receives from other nations.) At that time they had no control over individual governments' economic decisions and they did not have a license to intervene in national policy.

However, over the last 20 years the IMF and World Bank have joined forces with international "global free market" financiers to take more and more of the power over financial decisions such as budgets, currency, interest rates, and trade policies away from the people affected and away from national governments.

Although the World Bank in particular was formed to help poor nations develop, there is now a wider gap between the wealthy and the poor throughout the world than when these institutions were set up. In addition, instead of resources flowing from the wealthy countries to the poorer countries, there is actually a net transfer of resources from the poorer countries to the industrialized countries. According to UN secretary general Kofi Annan, "many poor countries

PI POINTER

The Philippines pays out $28 in debt service for every $1 received in aid grants. That makes it hard for the government to invest in health and education.

are so indebted that the net transfer of resources, in the form of interest and repayment, leads to a net outflow into industrialized countries instead of the other way around."[1] Many countries, especially in Africa, continue to sink deeper and deeper into debt to individual countries, private banks, and the World Bank.

According to Soren Ambrose of the 50 Years is Enough network, an international coalition of organizations formed on the 50th anniversary of the founding of the World Bank and IMF, "in most of a group of 83 poor countries that have received substantial IMF financing between 1978 and 1997, unemployment increased, real wages fell, income distribution became more unequal, poverty rose, food production per capita declined, external debt grew, and social expenditures were cut during those years." IMF and World Bank programs have also devastated healthcare systems in Africa, making people there more susceptible to the spread of HIV/AIDS.

Structural adjustment programs (SAPs) are conditions the IMF sets that developing countries must agree to if they want access to loans from industrialized countries and international trade institutions. These conditions include devaluing currency, reducing wages, privatizing state-owned industries, cutting social service employment, and cutting social spending. In addition, the developing countries' economies must be opened to foreign investment and must emphasize exports so that foreign currency can be used for servicing the debt. Countries are often caught in a catch-22. If they agree to the IMF conditions, their internal economies are weakened, but if they reject the conditions they remain impoverished, without access to financing.

The economic standing of women in developing countries has worsened under SAPs, partly because women still make up 70 percent of the world's poor. When scarce resources are diverted from education and healthcare to pay for the debt, it means women and girls have fewer educational opportunities, their health is threatened, and women face an increased burden as caregivers in the home and providers of formal or informal education. According to Peggy Antrobus of Development Alternatives with Women for a New Era (DAWN), "Underlying these policies (SAPs) is a set of assumptions about women's work: that women are housewives, do not work and therefore, that women can fill the gap created by cuts in social services ... The governments must not spend money on health, education, and human infrastructure, this must be left to the private sector or the household, meaning to women. The foundation is that women's time and labour can be exploited."[2]

In Zambia, for example, SAPs have meant that less money is spent on education. Since families currently pay most primary school costs, and since women are responsible for school fees, this means the bur-

UNHAPPY BIRTHDAY

On April 21, 2004, in a park across from the World Bank headquarters in Washington, DC, activists, students, and people of faith concerned about the impact of international debt on impoverished nations threw an "unhappy 60th birthday" party for the IMF and World Bank. They delivered to a representative of the World Bank the first shipment of more than 10,000 "unhappy birthday" cards signed and sent by citizens from 23 countries and more than 40 US states. The cards called on the institutions to cancel all debts of impoverished nations without imposing harmful conditions.

den of paying falls on them. On the African continent, where women produce three quarters of the food, SAP policies promoting exports forced women to devote their land and unpaid labor to export crop production. This shift has increased hunger and decreased per capita food production in the country. The SAPs and high debt levels have also had a serious impact on children. Prenatal care and health funds are often the first things cut from public budgets.

The World Bank and IMF policies are harmful to people around the world, but they also harm people in the United States. By enforcing draconian policies on countries so they can pay off their debts, the IMF helps to keep wages down in many countries. This in turn encourages corporations to move operations to those countries to use the cheaper labor, contributing to downward pressure on US wages. Lower wages in other countries, produced by IMF policies, reduce foreign demand for US-made goods, thereby endangering jobs and factories in the US

What is the connection between the institutions set up at Bretton Woods and the US national budget? Both the IMF and the World Bank are located in Washington, DC. Their budgets are structured so that US taxpayers pay a large portion of their expenses and loans. This means that US taxpayers are subsidizing the activities of these institutions, without fully understanding their missions or the impact they are having on others and on our own economy. The United States, because its financial contribution is the largest, carries the most weight in decisions of the institutions.

Globalization

Trade policies which the US took a lead in promoting also exemplify the harmful effects around the world. Following World War II, Western industrialized countries established international organizations to promote trade that would benefit the West. In 1947, 23 countries signed the General Agreement on Tariffs and Trade (GATT). GATT removed barriers to free trade, which sounds good but has resulted in a worsening position for smaller countries in the global economy. In 1994, GATT member nations signed an agreement to establish the World Trade Organization (WTO), which took over the activities of GATT. The WTO focuses on corporate-managed trade, economic efficiency, and short-term corporate profits. It gives the private sector a lot of control over economic policy, while social and environmental costs are borne by the public.

One problem with the WTO is that the rules it establishes for trade between nations supersede the laws of individual countries. The US Constitution grants Congress exclusive authority to set US trade policy, but the WTO overrides that power, which means that our elected representatives, and therefore the people, cannot make decisions on matters that affect our economy. According to Public

Citizen, WTO dispute settlement panels have ruled that US policies ranging from tax laws to antidumping measures and regulations to protect everything from clean air to sea turtles are illegal, and the US government has changed domestic policies to conform to many of these rulings. Certainly there are international standards and agreements that should supersede US laws (see the sidebar on CEDAW later in this chapter for information on some of the United Nations conventions, for instance) but it is always important to look at whose interests the overriding laws are supporting.

The North American Free Trade Agreement (NAFTA) was the next phase of trade agreements, negotiated in 1994 between the United States, Mexico, and Canada. Its purpose is to integrate the three countries' respective economies by lowering, and eventually removing, tariff barriers. According to the Economic Policy Institute, there has been a net loss of 766,000 jobs in the United States that can be directly attributed to the NAFTA.

There is a growing realization in this country that free trade policies are hurting US workers. Paul A. Samuelson, a Nobel Prize-winning economist and professor emeritus at the Massachusetts Institute of Technology, has questioned whether the global trade regime will end up helping the US economy, as free trade advocates claim. The loss of US jobs to call centers and computer programmers in China and India in particular — known as "outsourcing" — is the latest example of "job flights" (manufacturing and professional jobs leaving the country) that have forced US workers to take wage cuts. Using real-world terms, Samuelson explained in an interview that "being able to purchase groceries 20 percent cheaper at Wal-Mart does not necessarily make up for the wage losses."[3] The workers who are getting the jobs may be no better off if they are forced to work long hours for very low wages, or if they are employed in unsafe workplaces.

The evolution of global financial institutions and current global trade trends are all part of what has come to be known as globalization. Economic globalization is characterized by more freedom of trade and corporations' use of financial and legislative means to circumvent local and national laws and standards. The current era of globalization was promoted by a school of economic thought known as neo-liberalism.

JUBILEE 2000

The historic National Forum on Poverty Reduction took place in April 2000 in La Paz, Bolivia. It was the culmination of a nationwide dialogue that involved ordinary Bolivians in decisions on how to spend money released through debt cancellation. There were regional consultations throughout the country, and the people who attended them chose delegates to take their conclusions to the national forum.

Irene Tokarski, co-coordinator of the Bolivian Jubilee 2000 Campaign, said that it was "the biggest event of this kind that has ever taken place in Bolivia. In total, an amazing 4,000 participants and over 800 organizations participated ... The Bolivian Government must respond to this and take our collective voice into account."[4] The declaration issued at the end of the forum called for civil society to participate in drawing up and monitoring the country's debt-reduction strategy.

The Bolivian Jubilee 2000 Campaign is part of a worldwide campaign, Jubilee 2000, calling for cancellation of the debt of developing countries. Jubilee 2000 draws its inspiration from the book of Leviticus in the Hebrew Scriptures. According to Leviticus, every 50th year is a Year of Jubilee in which social inequities are rectified, slaves are freed, land is returned to original owners, and debts are cancelled. The Jubilee 2000 campaign is based on the premise that many of the debts of impoverished countries are unpayable and drain resources from healthcare, education and other socially beneficial programs. Since 1996, impelled in part by the massive Jubilee campaign, the World Bank and International Monetary Fund have been pursuing a new poverty-reduction strategy to reduce the debt of the world's poorest countries (the Heavily Indebted Poor Countries or HIPCs).

In her "Short History of Neo-Liberalism," political economist Susan George describes how the neo-liberals expanded from a tiny group, which formed at the University of Chicago around philosopher-economist Friedrich von Hayek and students like Milton Friedman, to a huge international network of foundations, institutes, research centers, publications, scholars, writers, and public relations companies that developed, packaged, and pushed their ideas. The "implication of competition as the central value of neo-liberalism is that the public sector must be brutally downsized because it does not and cannot obey the basic law of competing for profits or for market share," George writes. "Privatisation is one of the major economic transformations of the past twenty years. The trend began in Britain and has spread throughout the world."

Neo-liberalism also advocates moving money up the economic ladder, which has led to stock market bubbles, untold paper wealth for the few, and financial crises. We see the most recent US manifestation of this trend in the large tax breaks George W. Bush has given the wealthy.

PI POINTER

If income is redistributed towards the bottom 80 percent of society, it will be used for consumption and consequently benefit employment. If wealth is redistributed towards the top, where people already have most of the things they need, it will not go into the local or national economy, but to international stock markets.

Foreign Aid

One of the ways the US participates in the global economy is through foreign aid programs. The US national budget includes expenditures for foreign aid, which are among the discretionary expenses (see Chapter 2). This foreign aid goes to other countries and is in the form of money, food, economic aid, development assistance, military aid, and loans. The United States gives around $15 billion in foreign aid each year, or less than one percent of the budget.

Foreign aid became a regular part of the national budget following World War II. Since then it has been designed to meet political objectives of the US government and is not primarily based on the needs of most people in countries receiving the aid. In addition, the amount of US aid is small given the size of the country's budget and economy.

US foreign aid expenditures are a combination of military assistance and social and economic assistance. The criteria the government considers when it decides to send military aid are whether the country in question is friendly to the US government and to American business and corporate interests. The two countries that receive the most military and economic aid are Israel and Egypt, which are both

PI POINTER

In total funding, US foreign aid contributions rank fourth behind Japan, Germany, and France. As a percentage of gross national income, though, the US contribution ranks dead last among the 22 wealthiest nations, behind such countries as Portugal, New Zealand, and Ireland.

viewed as central to US strategic interests in the volatile Middle East. Much of US military aid money is used by the recipient country to buy US-made weapons or to set up its own weapon production.

US military aid contributes to a diversion of resources the country could be spending on education, housing, and healthcare, which has a direct negative impact on quality of life for women and their families. High levels of military aid also increase the likelihood of war, violence, and disruption of communities. A study by the Latin America Working Group Education Fund found that total US military aid to Latin America now almost equals the amount of money devoted to social or economic development there.[5]

In 1961 Congress passed the Foreign Assistance Act, creating the Agency for International Development (AID) to coordinate development aid, humanitarian assistance, food aid, and business-promotion programs. Although it sounded like a good thing, AID programs tended to create problems rather than addressing poverty or under-development in other countries. Aid went to regimes in Asia and Latin America that oppressed, or even tortured, their own citizens. Food aid often caused a country to become dependent on US goods instead of supporting local agriculture. Support that benefited US businesses often undermined local organizations trying to organize for better working conditions and grass-roots programs.

In the 1980s, foreign aid was used to subsidize private sector development in other countries. To ensure that business interests were supported, US aid was often linked to structural adjustment programs of the World Bank and IMF. This meant that many countries could not receive aid unless they made changes in their economy and budget that hurt the majority of the people.

In addition to the aid that goes from the United States to other countries (known as bilateral aid), there is also aid given in conjunction with other countries (multilateral aid), often through the United Nations. The UN, including all its agencies and funds, spends about $10 billion each year, or about $1.70 for each of the world's inhabitants. This is a very small sum compared to most government budgets, and it is a tiny fraction of the world's military spending. In recent years the UN has faced a financial crisis and has been forced to cut back on important programs in all areas. Many member states have not paid their full dues and have reduced their donations to the UN's voluntary funds. As of 2004, the United States alone owed $557 million — 53 percent of the UN's regular budget — even though a majority of Americans favor the US paying its UN dues in full. The United States has also failed to pay what it promised to support particular UN programs and now owes close to $1.5 billion for all international organizations, including the regular UN budget, UN peacekeeping, and several specialized UN agencies.

One UN agency that is of particular importance to women around the world, especially the poorest women, is the Population Fund (UNFPA), which provides family planning and reproductive health

THE CURRENCY TRANSACTION TAX

In the late 1980s, James Tobin, a Nobel laureate economist, proposed putting a sales tax on currency trades across national borders. Since then, activists and economists have taken up this concept and are campaigning for this tax to be enacted. The proposal would redirect a tiny portion of the $1.8 trillion a day that is traded in the volatile international currency market. Money from the tax would go to projects that address disease, poverty, hunger, debt, and environmental crises. If the tax took in 20 cents on the dollar, it would yield $150 billion annually.

The trade in currency is dominated by exchange rate speculations, which are short- and long-term profit-seeking transactions. Money managers buy and sell massive amounts of currency around the globe every day to seek profit from small fluctuations in value. This kind of speculation plays havoc with national budgets, economic planning, and allocation of resources. It can contribute to shockingly quick services. The UNFPA works to prevent 500,000 unwanted pregnancies and 200,000 abortions annually. The United States has contributed unevenly or not at all in recent years because conservatives in Congress claim the program supports abortion.

Gender Budgets Around the World

Women have responded to the globalization of the world economy by developing national budgets responsive to gender, poverty, and environmental issues. This movement gathered steam in September 1995 when 32,000 women from all over the world gathered in Beijing and Hairou, China, for the United Nations Non-Governmental Organization (NGO) Forum, which was held in conjunction with the Fourth World Conference on Women (the official UN governmental conference). The Forum was truly a "village of women," filled with the sights, sounds, energy, heartbreaking stories, and inspirational experiences of women from all parts of the globe. This was the largest UN gathering ever, and certainly the largest gathering of women in history.

I led a workshop at the NGO Forum on "Women's Budgets." Women came from many countries, including Denmark, Georgia, the United States, New Zealand, France, Canada, and Japan, to attend. One of the participants in the workshop — Keti Dolidze, a

currency devaluations for developing countries (such as happened to Mexico in 1994) and the increases in poverty and unemployment that result.

Many nongovernmental organizations, including the World Council of Churches, the AFL-CIO, and War on Want in Britain, are calling on national governments to enact a unilateral tax and then push for cooperation with other countries to produce a global tax. The Canadian government has voted in favor of the tax, 100 Brazilian parliamentarians have initiated a campaign to get parliamentarians around the world to support it, and the European parliament is considering it. The prime minister of Malaysia has said that "currency trading is unnecessary, unproductive, and totally immoral. It should be stopped. It should be made illegal."[6]

In July 2004, Belgium became the first country to enact legislation for a currency transaction tax.

Georgian actress, filmmaker, and aide to Georgian president Eduard Shevardnadze — revealed that it was difficult to think about what kind of budget her government should have, since they had virtually no income at the time. Many countries' budgets may be in crisis, or tax and expense figures may be unavailable to the public, but times of crisis or political change often provide an opening for new understanding of the budget challenges, and they may give women a chance to take a bigger role in determining priorities.

The increasing power of multinational corporations and their impact on women was a theme running through the conference. Of particular concern was the concentration of women in low-paying jobs with unsafe conditions, especially in the sweatshops and home work of the garment industry. Workers, primarily women, in the 130 poorest countries endure exploitative labor practices to provide goods for people in the 30 richest countries. In spite of these realities, there was tremendous excitement at the forum about women gaining "economic literacy" and working for a change in economic and budget policies at the national level. We also recognized the need to build our political and organizing capacity so that women could start setting the agenda for all aspects of national budgets. Several women pointed out that, at Beijing, many women from the United States got a real education about how important their country and the US budget are in the lives of women all over the world.

At the end of the conference, delegates from 189 countries unanimously adopted the Beijing Declaration and a Platform for Action to improve the status of women worldwide. Although these documents are not binding, they indicate an international consensus on key issues affecting women. The countries that signed agreed to implement recommendations on a range of issues as they concerned women, from poverty, health and education to armed conflict, the media, and the environment. You can read the full text of the Beijing Declaration and the Platform for Action on the UN website <www.un.org/womenwatch/daw/beijing/platform/index.html>.

The platform includes the following strategic objectives for national governments related to women and budgets:

1. Restructure and target the allocation of public expenditures to promote women's economic opportunities and equal access to

productive resources and to address the basic social education and health needs of women.

2. Facilitate more open and transparent budget processes.
3. Review, adopt, and maintain macroeconomic policies and development strategies that address the needs and efforts of women in poverty.

In addition, the document states that

> the primary responsibility for implementing the strategic objectives of the Platform for Action rests with Governments. To achieve these objectives, Governments should make efforts to systematically review how women benefit from public sector expenditures; adjust budgets to ensure equality of access to public sector expenditures, both for enhancing productive capacity and for meeting social needs; and achieve the gender-related commitments made in other United Nations summits and conferences. To develop successful national implementation strategies for the Platform for Action, Governments should allocate sufficient resources, including resources for undertaking gender-impact analysis. Governments should also encourage non-governmental organizations and private sector and other institutions to mobilize additional resources.

These strategic objectives, combined with increasing gender- and class-based critiques of economic and development policy among NGOs, have encouraged women to focus on and organize around budget processes and content in many countries. The United Nations Development Program and UNIFEM, the United Nations women's fund, have worked to coordinate a wide range of gender-sensitive, pro-poor, pro-environment budget initiatives. They have held conferences for budget practitioners from around the world. Participants at the conferences were from academia, civil society organizations, UN agencies, and governments, illustrating the broad range of involvement and strategies now being brought to budget work.

In addition, in a major international campaign, UNIFEM, the Commonwealth Secretariat (the primary coordinating agency of the 54 member governments of the Commonwealth), and the International Development Research Center (IDRC) in Canada are cosponsoring a campaign to get all countries to incorporate gender analysis into their national budget processes by 2015. Noeleen Heyzer, executive director of UNIFEM, has said that "ignoring the gender impact of the budget is not neutrality. It is blindness. And blindness has a high human and economic cost: lower productivity; lower development of people's capacity and lower levels of well being."[7]

According to UNIFEM, gender-responsive budgets promote:

❖ Equality: Gender equality becomes a goal and an indicator of economic governance. Governments and NGOs can use CEDAW (see sidebar) and other human rights instruments to see if the rights of women are being promoted in public budgeting.

❖ Accountability: Countries are held to the commitments they made in international agreements because the budget makes national priorities and the effects of decisions clear.

❖ Efficiency: Gender inequality is bad economic and social policy, slowing development and productivity for the country as a whole.

❖ Transparency: More open, participatory, and responsive budgets engage more people in crucial economic and budget decisions.

CEDAW

The Convention on the Elimination of All Forms of Discrimination Against Women (CEDAW) is the most comprehensive and detailed international treaty to date that addresses the rights of women. It was adopted by the UN General Assembly in 1979 and entered into force in 1981, bringing to a climax UN efforts to codify international legal standards for women.

President Jimmy Carter signed this human rights treaty in 1980, and it was sent to the US Senate Foreign Relations Committee for ratification. Despite tremendous pressure from many organizations and prominent individuals in the United States since then — including Hillary Rodham Clinton and President Bill Clinton when they were in the White House — ratification is still pending. The United States made ratification of CEDAW by the year 2000 one of its public commitments at the UN Fourth World Conference on Women but was unable to achieve that. As of 2004, 177 countries — over 90 percent of the members of the United Nations — are party to the Convention.

Women have been often left out of these decisions, so opening up the budget processes and decisions is crucial for encouraging full civic participation.

The South African Women's Budget Initiative (WBI) has been one of the most inspiring women's budget efforts, involving both NGOs and parliamentarians since 1995. Each year they do a gender analysis of the budget from both inside and outside the government. The budget studies contain analyses of taxation, public sector employment, and the budget process and have contributed to gender-sensitive economic theory. The WBI has also developed case studies from local budgets and produced grass-roots budget literacy materials.

Debbie Budlender, who has worked with the WBI, emphasizes that "even parliamentarians have limited say in budget matters. The WBI has strengthened gender advocacy in the country. But the advocacy has been strong because it has been based firmly on the understanding that budgets do not stand alone — that while no policy can be effective without an adequate budget, similarly budgetary battles can only be won if they are waged on the basis of the policies and principles underlying them."

By accepting the Convention, states commit to end discrimination against women in all forms, by implementing a series of measures, including the following:

- Incorporate the principle of equality of men and women in the legal system, abolish all discriminatory laws, and adopt laws prohibiting discrimination against women
- Establish tribunals and other public institutions to ensure women are effectively protected from discrimination
- Work to end all acts of discrimination against women by persons, organizations, or enterprises

The Convention provides the basis for realizing equality between women and men by ensuring women's equal access to, and equal opportunities in, political and public life — including the right to vote and to stand for election — as well as education, health, and employment. States that are party to the Convention agree to take all appropriate measures, including legislation and temporary special measures, so that women can enjoy all their human rights and fundamental freedoms.

This reminds us how important it is for women to get involved in reinventing economics so that it reflects the reality of women's lives and contributes to equity for everyone. We also should not forget that countries are forming their budgets in the context of larger macroeconomic policies, so efforts to change budgets benefit from being connected to the fight to change global economic policies.

The first women's budgets were produced in Australia in the mid-1980s. They were the inspiration for several of the current initiatives. Gender-responsive budgeting is happening all over the world now, including in Sri Lanka, Bangladesh, Russia, Brazil, Mexico, Peru, Chile, and India.

PART 3

Creating the Future

WE ARE NOW ON THE THIRD PART OF OUR JOURNEY into the land of the national budget. As public investigators, we have shed light on some mysteries about the budget. As we learned in Part One, the national budget represents the receipt and allocation of abundant resources that belong to the people of the United States. In Part Two we learned that the national budget is embedded in and affects a wide range of national and international economic patterns and policies. In Part Three we will do two things: look at the values, guiding principles, and frameworks that could be used to create a new, gender-responsive budget for the United States; and learn about actions we can take and resources we can use to address budget and economic issues. This section of the book is called "Creating the Future" because the future is open and subject to our influence.

CHAPTER 8

❖

A New Budget
for the United States

Law is always someone's desire — it is always the
desire of the powerful: let's demonstrate this desire,
let's make our desire become law too!
— Augusto Boal, *Legislative Theater*

EVERY CHILD GOES TO BED SAFE, HEALTHY, AND WELL-NOURISHED.
Everyone learns preventive healthcare, and various methods of
treating injury and disease are available to all. Births take place in a
warm, gently lighted, peaceful, drug-free environment. Every teenager
and adult contributes his or her unique talents to the community,
takes part in the educational resources of the community as desired,
and has access to paid employment that meets financial needs. Support
services for families, such as childcare, paid family leave, and after-
school programs, are all available. The elderly are respected for their
wisdom and cared for with grace and love. Every family, no matter
what its configuration, has a properly heated and cooled home
with plenty of room for its members. Food is plentiful, healthy, and
everyone has enough. Political participation skills are taught and
practiced everywhere, and anyone can afford to run for public office.
There is a participatory process for determining how community
and national resources will be used. People from other countries
come freely to visit, and they welcome us warmly to their countries.
We are partners with every other country in the world to make sure
that all people have their needs met, safety is provided for all

DREAMSTORM: CREATING THE VISION

Seventeen women sit in a circle in a room at Boston City Hall. The women in the room are students, activists, staff members of organizations.[1] It is a hot day in July 1997. We build our energy together and begin to imagine what our national budget and national economic policies could be if they met our deep needs. We call out the visions that come up for us as we allow ourselves to enter the Dreamstorm, a combination of brainstorming and dreaming about future possibilities.

- Publicly funded elections
- Moratorium on prisons
- Tax deductions for using sustainable transportation
- Natural resources reflected as assets in budget accounting
- Reduction in funding to the International Monetary Fund (IMF) and the World Bank
- Guaranteed livable wage
- Democratically selected council of national economic advisors
- Guaranteed housing for all
- Paid maternity and family leave
- Programs to build self-esteem for and empower young people

- National healthcare system so everyone is covered
- Recognition in tax and accounting structures of the wealth built on unwaged work
- Foreign aid that addresses the true community-based needs of people in other countries
- Special tax on arms manufacturer and exporters to pay for social programs
- Restructuring of public education system in inner cities
- Debt relief for countries in Africa, Asia, and Latin America

When the group took another step and prioritized these budget/economic policies, the top issues were those related to guaranteeing adequate income; providing better public education, healthcare and wellness; progressive tax structures; and paid maternity and family leave.

We also did a Dreamstorm for the state budget of Massachusetts and related economic policies. Some of the following visions came up:

- No more tax breaks for Raytheon and Fidelity
- Restore the capital gains tax

- Divest state funds from banks that invest in armaments
- Provide adequate state subsidies for housing

- Provide free higher education
- Allocate more money for mass transit

- Cancel the real estate tax exemption for private universities and hospitals

There were many more ideas that came up during our Dreamstorm, but this gives you an idea of the breadth of concerns and passions. One woman liked that this was "gut-informed" not "head-informed." We all know in our gut what is most important to us, and if we don't get too much into thinking about it, we know at a deep level what would reflect that nationally. What comes out in a Dreamstorm also reflects how our values might appear in policy. We felt the power of being in a place of possibility, thinking about what we wanted rather than what we didn't want. The power that will create a new budget comes from dwelling in that place of compelling vision that brings together the perspectives and experiences of a variety of women.

One student at a Dreamstorm at Smith College told the story of her father, who died because of inadequate healthcare when he needed it. To her, national healthcare was something that her heart, trained by her experience, demanded. Millions of people in the United States have experienced this lack of good healthcare and share in her desire to throw out a net so that no more people have to suffer from a lack of healthcare in a land of plenty.

The concept of the Dreamstorm was created by another group of women representing a wide variety of organizations who gathered in October 1996.[2] They met at the Jane Addams House, a woman-owned building that is the national headquarters of the US section of the Women's International League for Peace and Freedom (WILPF).

That meeting continued for three days, taking us deep into the implications of changing the budget and economic policies. We dreamed specific things we wanted in the national budget and in national economic policies, similar to those brought forward at the Boston meeting. As we were brainstorming, someone pointed out that we were brainstorming and dreaming at the same time. Thus was born the Dreamstorm.

The Dreamstorm taps into life knowledge and passion, and creates a powerful vision that is the first step to having an impact on the future direction of the United States. Several Dreamstorms conducted by the Women's Budget Project helped develop the values, guiding principles, and structure for the new budget that are contained in this chapter.

through international cooperation, and the ecosystem and other species are protected.

As PIs, we have looked into the mysteries of the current national budget and learned that we have the resources to make this vision for our country a reality. As we consider the content of a new budget for the United States that will meet the needs of all people, the central question is: How do we want to gather and use our common resources as a nation, both for ourselves and as part of a global community and web of life? We have learned that the national budget does not exist in a vacuum; it is a powerful part of the national and global economy and a reflection of values and priorities. Rethinking the budget can be one tool to move the country in a different direction.

Values, Guiding Principles, and Structure

First we need to decide what values, guiding principles, and budget structure would meet the needs of women and all people in the United States. The suggested values, guiding principles, and structure I describe here were developed by women who participated in workshops and consultations organized by the Women's Budget Project in the 1990s. Women at these sessions used a "Dreamstorm" process to tap into their visions and values (see sidebar below).

Values Underlying the New Budget
* Interdependence: All life is sacred and all people contribute to, receive from, and are fully interdependent with the human community and the Earth's resources.
* Abundance: There is an abundance of financial resources, human creativity, and cooperative energy available for meeting all challenges.
* Democracy: True participatory democracy in which the people, not corporations, are in charge is essential for setting national priorities and social and economic policies.

Guiding Principles for the New Budget
The following principles will guide the creation of a budget that meets the needs of all people. Realizing this vision may require

economic policies rather than a direct infusion of funds, but it indicates what reality should look like after the new budget is implemented.

❖ Commitment to meet the basic human needs of all people for food, housing, healthcare, education, protection from violence, jobs at good wages, and adequate social safety nets for those who can't work.

❖ Equitable distribution of the nation's resources, income, and wealth.

❖ Financial self-sufficiency for women and people of color, as well as the full development of young people.

❖ Peace-directed foreign policy, with an emphasis on working within multilateral institutions such as United Nations bodies and agencies, and the International Criminal Court.

❖ Public life and discourse that are democratic, welcome diversity, and dismantle discrimination based on race, ethnicity, gender, age, class, ability, and sexual orientation.

❖ Support of the variety of economic, cultural, spiritual, and artistic expression of communities.

❖ Harmony with ecological processes and sustainability of natural resources.

These principles create a framework in which we can think about and produce a new national budget and economic policies. They will also help guide us through a transition from the old budget to the new one. For example, in the old budget paradigm, the concept of scarcity is an overriding feature. If we believe that scarcity is real, the possibilities shrink and we can come to believe that not much change is possible. A belief in abundance, however, opens the door to many different outcomes: anything is possible.

According to *Webster's Dictionary,* the Latin word "unda," which means "wave," is the root of the word "abundance." The preposition "ab" in Latin means, among other possibilities, "on" or "as a result of." Waves are ever-renewing and ever-forming, whether they are ocean waves or waves of electrical vibrations or human energy. This echoes the metaphor of the river we used to think about income and expenses in Chapters 2 and 3. What streams do you want to feed into our mighty river of national resources? In which directions and for what purposes do you want the resources to flow back out?

Figure 8.1 compares the paradigms of the old budget and the new budget.

Old Budget vs. New Budget Contributions

The old budget contributes to:	The new budget contributes to:
Survival of isolated individuals and communities	Individuals and communities thriving and interdependent
Scarcity of community resources (economic and non-economic)	Abundance of community resources (economic and non-economic)
Corporate subsidies from public resources	Public resources invested in community needs
Women's financial dependence	Women's financial self-sufficiency
Ecological destruction	Ecological sustainability
Inequitable distribution of resources	Equitable distribution of resources
Militarism/war/violence	Human rights, demilitarization, peaceful resolution of conflict
Racism/patriarchy/class system	Inclusion/democracy/justice

figure 8.1

Structure for the New Budget

These values, principles, and new paradigm demand a new vision and structure for the budget itself in order to make it transparent and understandable, and to create a context for incorporating the values and guiding principles. The Women's Budget Project also developed the structure suggested in Figure 8.2. This structure makes explicit the larger context for creating national budgets that are equitable and meet the needs of all the people in the United States.

We are obviously far from having this structure for the budget right now, but it provides a vision of where we want to get to and will help us create strategies for moving in this direction. This is not an attempt to put together an annual national budget, with line-by-line taxation and expenses, but rather an alternative method of budget presentation that changes the way the budget is formulated, developed, presented, and evaluated. Annual budgets with line-by-line program funding can then be prepared within the context of this structure.

Structure for the New Budget for the United States

Income (Contributions/Resources)	Expenses (Investments/Responsibilities)	Capital Budget (Long-Term Investments)	Surplus/Debt/National Wealth (Assets/Liabilities)
Examples:	*Examples:*	*Examples:*	*Examples:*
• Progressive income tax	• Housing	• National health insurance (all people covered)	• Surplus (if any in given year)
• Tax on corporate profits	• Community health care	• Social security	• Deficit (if any in given year)
• Payroll tax for social security	• Education, including Head Start	• Reparations for slavery and for Native Americans	• National wealth, including land, financial assets such as gold and mortgages, physical assets, research and development capital, education capital
• Tax breaks for low-income working parents	• Nutrition, including Women, Infants and Children (WIC) program	• Education infrastructure	• Public debt
• Other taxes/tax breaks	• Child care	• Public transportation infrastructure	• Social and economic indicators
• Include value of unpaid home and community economic contribution	• Employment and training	• Housing infrastructure for low-income people	• Gender and race impact analysis
• Include underlying value of earth/ecosystem	• Community development	• Public infrastructure: roads, bridges, sewer, water systems	• Environmental sustainability indicators
	• Transportation	• Research and development	• International indicators
	• Clean water		
	• Clean air		
	• Sustainable energy		
	• Regional/state and local support		
	• Gender specific initiatives such as violence against women programs		
	• Paid family leave		
	• Public safety and security		
	• Military spending		
	• Disarmament initiatives		
	• United Nations and other international program contributions		
	• Foreign Aid		
	• Peacemaking training		
	• Public financing of elections		
	• Popular education in democracy skills		
	• National government administrative expenses		

Structure for the New Budget for the United States (cont'd)

Key Related Economic/Social Policies	
• Affirmative Action	• Labor policy
• Pay equity implementation	• Native American land and tribal issues
• Immigration policy	• Foreign/international policy
• Monetary policy	• Defense/human security policy
• Trade policy	• Corporate governance
• Wage policy	

figure 8.2

This new budget structure includes aspects of gender-responsive and inclusive budgeting practices such as the following:

❖ It measures the care economy in the budget statement and accounting.

❖ It uses government-conducted time-use studies and other data collection to calculate the value of unpaid work.

❖ It includes indicators of the budget's impacts on gender and race.

❖ It includes the environmental costs of programs in the accounting.

❖ It uses internationally recognized social and economic indicators for part of the budget evaluation, such as the Human Development Index and the Gender-Related Development Index.

❖ It uses the Environmental Sustainability Index (see Chapter 6 for more about these indexes).

❖ It carries out a gender audit preceding and following budget decisions on tax and expense allocations. The following are some of the questions to ask in a gender audit:

• How does taxation policy affect women?

• Who is the intended beneficiary of each budget line?

• Who needs the service funded by each budget line?

• Who will actually benefit from the service?

• Who will provide the service?

• Who will find employment thanks to the budget line?

• Will the budget line benefit disadvantaged groups?

• How will the budget affect the care economy?

• Are there better alternatives to each budget line?

❖ It includes a review of the provisions of CEDAW, the Beijing Platform for Action, the Convention on the Elimination of All Forms of Racial Discrimination (CERD), and the Convention on the Rights of the Child, to ensure the budget provides for the human rights of all.

❖ It ensures the full participation of women in the development, evaluation, and implementation of the national budget, addressing the following questions:

- What are the obstacles to women fully participating in budgeting at all levels, and how can these be addressed in ways that move change in the direction of implementing key policies?

- What are the pressure points where community-based women can presently participate in the budgeting process at local, state, and federal levels?

- Who are the organizational and individual allies who can enhance women's participation?

❖ It uses the Gender Empowerment Measure (GEM) to compare the US budget to budgets of other countries The GEM is a composite indicator that captures gender inequality in three key areas:

- Political participation and decision making, as measured by women's and men's percentage shares of parliamentary [congressional] seats

- Economic participation and decision-making power, as measured by two indicators: women's and men's percentage shares of positions as legislators, senior officials, and managers; and women's and men's percentage shares of professional and technical positions

- Power over economic resources

❖ It uses the Family Self-Sufficiency Standard in place of traditional poverty measures.

Because women are currently concentrated in lower-paying jobs, with less income and wealth than men, and bearing more responsibility for family service tasks, including childcare and elder care, it means that national budgetary and related economic policies can have a disproportionate impact on their financial position. Certain policies are particularly important to women's overall financial well-being, and it is crucial that they are implemented within the new budget or as supporting economic policies. These key policies include the following elements:

- Equal pay/comparable worth implementation
- Work and family benefits, such as paid leave, childcare, control over work hours
- National healthcare
- Retirement security
- Training and education for jobs at good wages
- Increase in public sector jobs
- Affordable housing
- Tax reform to assist women's self-sufficiency
- Increase in unionization and work-related benefits

Strategies for Creating the New Budget

The following strategies suggest some of the ways we can begin to create a new US budget that takes into account the current budget's impact on gender and race.

1. Provide a research base, do data and indicator development, and incorporate gender responsiveness into budgetary practice.

One of the most important things we need as we create a new budget is a basis of information that will help us decide how to make the collection of taxes and the allocation of resources more equitable. After we have this information, we can begin to look at specific numbers for taxation and investment that will be gender responsive. Because women of color can experience several levels of discrimination in the budget, we also need to determine how to collect data showing race-based inequities in taxation and budget expenditures.

In an article they wrote for *Public Administration Review*, Marilyn Marks Rubin and John R. Bartle call for gender budgeting to become a budget reform in the United States, following a long line of similar efforts such as planning programming budget systems (PPBS), management by objectives (MBO), zero-based budgeting (ZBB), target-based budgeting (TBB), and performance budgeting. They believe that gender inequities in the budget can be addressed by starting with the audit/evaluation phase of the budget cycle, as most gender budget initiatives around the world have done.

According to Rubin and Bartle, "a full-fledged gender budget would require measuring expenditure incidence for all functions of government from fire protection to higher education to clean water to national defense. Ultimately, gender analysis would have to be at the program level and would require a detailed examination of the incidence of each program in each function. After enough analysis was completed, it would enable comparisons of the gender impact of programs."

In addition, we have to decide how to measure the care economy and how to relate it to the budgetary accounting and process. In an interview with Cathy Cavanaugh, Marilyn Waring (author of *Counting for Nothing*) pointed out that the Australian government has been able to demonstrate that household production is the single largest productive sector of the Australian economy. It exceeds the value of all manufacturing by a multiple of ten, and the value of all mining and mineral extraction by a multiple of three. Obviously this can affect the allocation and distribution of public funds and has implications for labor, wage, job training, and family-friendly national policies.

2. Mobilize women and men to get involved in opening up the budget process at all levels, and collect best practices.

Budget transparency can be a powerful tool and motivator for change. When people see how their public resources are being used at all levels of government, when they see what programs are available and better understand the decision-making process, they're more likely to be inspired to redirect those resources and/or get new decision makers into office. (See the sidebar on the experiment at the city level in Porto Alegre, Brazil.)

The more we become familiar with and understand budgets and budget processes, the easier it will be for us to demand gender responsiveness at all levels, including the national government. Issues of transparency and accountability exist at every level of government — city, county, state, and federal — and there are various levels of public scrutiny around the country and throughout the world.

3. Change the federal poverty measure and replace it with the Family Self-Sufficiency Standard or another standard based on the actual cost of living and taking into account a variety of factors.

The federal poverty measure was developed in the 1960s, when families looked very different — there are many more households headed by a single parent today. In addition, families spend more of their income on housing, healthcare, and transportation than they used to, and less on food. Families also spend more on certain items, like childcare, due to the increased number of women in the labor force. The poverty measure needs to be revised to take all of this into account.

The poverty measure is important because it can determine what government-funded programs, at what level of support, people can access. This is a particularly urgent issue for women who head households on their own and generally have lower wages and fewer benefits.

Unlike the federal poverty standard, the Self-Sufficiency Standard (described in Chapter 3) accounts for the costs of living and working according to family size/composition and geographic location. The standard defines the amount of income necessary to meet basic needs (including paying taxes) in the regular "marketplace" without public subsidies (such as public housing, food stamps, Medicaid, or childcare) or private/informal subsidies (such as free babysitting by a relative or friend, food provided by churches or local food banks, or shared housing). It estimates the level of income necessary for a given family type — whether working now or making the transition to work — to be independent of welfare and/or other public and private subsidies.

The standard guides policy makers and program providers as they decide how to target their education, job training, workforce development, and welfare-to-work resources. It also shows policy makers how subsidizing childcare, transportation, or healthcare affects the amount of wages working families need to make ends meet.

4. Promote Senate ratification of CEDAW and adherence to other key international human rights conventions.

The Senate still has not ratified the Convention on the Elimination of Discrimination Against Women (CEDAW). This is an important human rights treaty, as it affects over half of the world's population.

It sets standards that will be crucial to ensure that all government laws and regulations, including national budgets, are in accord with international antidiscrimination statutes.

The San Francisco Commission on the Status of Women has brought CEDAW down to the municipal level. In April 1998, San Francisco became the first city in this country to adopt an ordinance implementing CEDAW locally. It also established a task force that works with the commission and city departments to identify discrimination against women and girls and to implement human rights principles.

In addition to CEDAW, other important UN conventions for women and girls include the Convention on the Elimination of All Forms of Racial Discrimination (CERD), the International Covenant on Economic, Social and Cultural Rights (CESCR), and the Convention on the Rights of the Child (CRC). For most women, the intersection of race and gender are crucial to understanding and dealing with the barriers to full economic and social equality and flourishing. These conventions are important tools for education — everyone must know what rights they have — and for advocacy — to ensure governments are following internationally agreed upon standards of human rights.

5. Monitor US government progress on implementing Beijing Platform for Action recommendations on budgeting and economic policy.

Countries will be coming together in 2005 to celebrate 10 years of the Beijing Platform for Action, to discuss plans for another World Conference on Women, and to evaluate global progress towards the mandates in the Platform for Action. We need a high-level government commission to review the progress the country has made towards implementing the objectives set out in the Platform for Action from the Fourth World Conference on Women, especially in the areas of budgeting and economic policy. Such a commission could monitor progress, as well as recommend how government agencies and Congress can incorporate the platform into goals and processes. We need to make the case for how a gender-impact analysis of the budget will benefit society at large, as well as fulfill our commitments to people from other countries.

6. Re-establish the President's Interagency Council on Women and the Office of Women's Initiatives and Outreach in the White House and end the downgrading of women's concerns at the administration level.

President George W. Bush has shown a direct disregard for the continued economic and social progress of women. According to the National Council for Research on Women (NCRW), in the first Bush term the administration deleted and altered information on women's issues that was posted on government agency websites. NCRW believes the deletion of information on subjects including pay equity and childcare was done to advance a political agenda. At least 25 publications have been removed from the website of the Department of Labor's Women's Bureau alone.

The NCRW reported that key government offices such as the Office of Women's Initiatives and Outreach in the White House and the President's Interagency Council on Women have been disbanded. The President's Interagency Council on Women was established in 1995 to ensure US implementation of the Platform for Action from the Fourth World Conference on Women. The council consisted of high-level representatives from federal agencies working together to develop policies and programs for the advancement of women and girls within the government, and to do public education and outreach. The Office of Women's Initiatives and Outreach served as a liaison between the White House and women's organizations, listening to women's concerns and proposals and bringing these ideas to the president and others in the administration. Its staff reviewed legislation and administration proposals to gauge their impact on women and make recommendations.

7. Work for election and campaign finance reform.

In order for democracy to have any meaning, people need to be involved in decisions about how their resources are collected and disbursed. Our current political system is distorted by the huge amount of money going to members of Congress and the high cost of running for office. If we are going to insure more diverse representation and the full rights of every voter, we will need to change the current electoral system. There are many proposals for changes, from electoral college reform to national funding of parties and congressional elections. (See resources in Chapter 9.)

PARTICIPATORY BUDGETS — PORTO ALEGRE

An experiment in participatory budgeting has been unfolding in a city in Brazil for fifteen years. Porto Alegre, a city the size of Boston, has been using participatory budgeting to determine municipal priorities and public investment. As of 2005, 50,000 people are participating in the process.

In 1989 the newly elected Workers Party mayor was committed to giving people a say in the way resources were distributed. He wanted the process to be participatory, rather than consultative. This means that all constituencies in the city participated in the actual decisions, and their voices were present in the discussions leading up to the decisions. The commitment to participation extended to those living in the poorest areas of the city, who had been totally left out of the city in terms of services.

The Workers Party initiated participatory budgeting to make the budget process transparent and also to let people have a say in how limited public funds were distributed. Mayoral resources had to be committed for organizing the communities, insuring that this process became a reality.

In order to maximize participation, the city is divided into regions and large regional meetings — called plenaries — are organized. Each year, everyone is invited to attend their regional plenary, and each constituency is invited to have a certain number of representatives at the meetings. The highest turnout has been in the poorest areas, since they have the most to gain from a change in municipal priorities. Each plenary sends representatives to the citywide meeting. They are required to vote the way the regional plenary had decided and to report back on the outcome. The votes in the citywide meeting set the priorities for the annual municipal budget.

This process has resulted in more productivity, less corruption, and more accountability on the part of public workers and officials. Although critics have charged that it helps to re-enforce business as usual, participatory budgeting has clearly been effective as a tool for organizing and mobilizing communities and has increased the technical understanding of community members.

Some form of participatory budget process has now been initiated in 100 municipalities throughout Brazil. The process has also become a best practice in public administration case study internationally.

CHAPTER 9

❖

What You Can Do

NOW THAT WE HAVE UNCOVERED some of the mysteries of the national budget and reflected on the values, principles, and structure for a new budget and economic policies for the United States, it is time to move into action. In this chapter I suggest some ways you can become involved in working on the national budget and economic issues, and I list resources for further investigation and action.

Working on the budget and economic issues can be overwhelming. You'll feel it's too big to get your head or your hands around. When this happens, take a deep breath and focus on the following questions:

❖ What is one thing you *can* get your hands around, that means something within the context of your own life?

❖ How do you use your skills and talents to have an impact on that one thing, however large or small?

Every change begins with small steps taken by ordinary people. The giant Social Security program began after workers and the unemployed marched, walked off the job, staged sit-ins in factories, endured violence, and fought for a broad social agenda. The government-sponsored pension that was enacted, as well as things like child labor laws and minimum wage laws, though imperfect, have made a difference for millions of people.

Civil rights laws were passed after thousands of small actions in southern communities — in large part led by women — gained momentum, and the government had to respond. Women earned the right to vote after decades of many women holding to the vision, taking step after step, not getting discouraged by harsh treatment, and organizing new women to work on the campaign. There is a dynamic connection between local and community actions and nationally coordinated campaigns, and all of them are needed.

Women and men all over the world are working to make their national and local budgets more transparent and accountable. They are holding out a vision for what the public sphere can and should provide for the people to whom it belongs. The huge size of the US budget and economy pose a special challenge, but the principle is the same: start weaving the threads and the pattern will take shape.

We are weaving a beautiful giant tapestry. We know the overall theme and the colors we want to emphasize, but the tapestry will only become a reality if each of us picks up a thread to work on and gives it our full attention, seeing the intricate overall pattern later. We don't know how the images in the tapestry will come together until we are into the work. For now, decide what thread you want to pick up, focus on that, and see where it takes you. I've provided questions and exercises in this chapter to help you find your thread if you don't already know what it is, or if you want to rethink your thread or renew your energy for what you are already doing.

The best way to decide which thread you should take up is to see what is right in front of you, what you care about, what you are drawn to do. Then you will start to see how you can connect with others who also want to do that work. There is no right or wrong way to do the work, and often fresh energy and insight move the work forward in ways that sticking to the same strategy cannot. On the other hand, it can be helpful to find out what others have already done and learned and to join with larger movements for change.

One of the things that becomes obvious when you look at history is that it has often been difficult to work across the lines of class and race in the United States. Sometimes the strategies the women's movement pursued did not include issues that were of central concern to women of color and low-income women. Sometimes it did not stand up against racism. If you take the time to reflect on how race and class have affected all of us, and if you make an effort to go outside your comfort levels, you can ultimately take effective action that will make a deeper difference in the long run. (I've listed some resources that can help you with these explorations.)

Taking Action

Taking action is always more fun and more effective if you join with others, though there are always many things you can do on your own as well. Taking action can take as little or as much time as you can spare or want to invest — the important thing is to be participating and working towards your vision of how you want things to be. I've listed just a few of the possibilities for action below:

- ❖ Join an organization (see the resource list for lots of possibilities)
- ❖ Volunteer with an organization
- ❖ Donate to an organization
- ❖ Start an organization
- ❖ Gather a group
- ❖ Bring undo-racism training to your community
- ❖ Take action against something in your community you want to change
- ❖ Start a cross-class group
- ❖ Hold a workshop about the economy for your community and/or train yourself in economic and budget literacy
- ❖ Put on a Legislative Theater event (see sidebar) in your community to illuminate the key issues
- ❖ Share success stories, gather links to resources, ask questions, give feedback about *Women and the US Budget*, and participate in an online Dreamstorm (what do you want to see in the national budget and related economic policies?) at <www.womenandtheus budget.com>.
- ❖ Set up a Budget Literacy and Action Group to work with this book
- ❖ Analyze your city or state budget and take action
- ❖ Contact your congressperson about economic and budget issues that concern you
- ❖ Contact your state representatives, senators, city councilors, and mayor about budget and economic issues that concern you
- ❖ Write letters to the editor
- ❖ Call in to talk shows
- ❖ Run for office

❖ Contribute to people running for office

❖ Volunteer for people running for office.

LEGISLATIVE THEATER

Theater director, playwright, author, and founder of the international movement of "Theater of the Oppressed," Augusto Boal was elected to the city council of Rio de Janeiro, Brazil, from 1993 to 1996. With his theater colleagues, he developed a program to teach Theater of the Oppressed to various communities within Rio — teachers, doctors, workers, students, farmers, and domestic servants. The purpose was to encourage people to act out their community's needs and wants. They created plays that addressed the concerns of the group and presented various solutions to the problems. This process is now known as Legislative Theater.

Using Legislative Theater, people from different communities and constituencies developed 13 laws that addressed their issues. These laws were then written and passed by the Parliament. Boal writes, "We do not accept that the elector [voter] should be a mere spectator to the actions of the parliamentarian, even when these actions are right. We want the electors to give their opinions, to discuss the issues, to put counter-arguments, we want them to share the responsibility for what their parliamentarian does." This process is now being used in several countries to help communities and constituencies clarify their needs and priorities and translate them into the policy-making arena.

Questions and Exercises

The following questions and exercises are designed to help you expand your awareness of how the issues raised in Women and the US Budget affect you. The more we can understand the impact of money and resource distribution at all levels of our lives, the more we can take our full power. Read through the following questions and exercises and do the ones that stand out for you. It can be helpful to do them with a friend or to get a group together. If you want to start a Budget Literacy and Action Group to read and discuss the book, or do the exercises together, and move into action, contact me through <www.womenandtheusbudget.com>.

Reflection Questions

❖ What caught your attention as you read *Women and the US Budget*?

❖ What did you notice in the book that affects you, that you care about, or that you know is important to you or those you love?

❖ Is there a particular issue that tugs at you and that you want to investigate more deeply?

❖ What made you angry/sad/excited?

Economic Life Story

❖ Write down (or tell a friend) your life story, using money and class as the focal point. Some things to consider:

• How did your family deal with/think about money?

• What has your relationship with money been like?

• What are the positives and negatives of the economic class you were born into/the class you are in now?

• How do you think being a woman has shaped your economic life story?

• What would you like the next chapter of your economic life story to be?

Personal Budget Overview

1) Where does your money come from?

• Write down all your sources of income (for example, salary, fees, public assistance, Social Security, disability payments, interest, dividends gifts, loans) and how much they totaled last year.

• Notice and make a note of which of these income sources are connected to the national budget or government.

• Are you able, as a woman, to build the financial life that you want and that would support you in the event of a separation, divorce, death of a spouse, disability of yourself or a spouse, need to care for an elderly parent or relative, or retirement?

2) Where does your money go?

• Write down all your expenses, dividing them into mandatory — those things you have to pay every month — and discretionary.

• Write down the taxes you pay (if any) or the tax expenditure programs you use, such as home mortgage tax deduction or Earned Income Tax Credit.

3) Debt or surplus?

- Write down all the things that fill out your economic picture, including debts you owe, debts people owe to you, assets you have (i.e., real estate, stocks and bonds, savings).
- If you have debt: Do you have a plan in place to repay that debt? Do you save at the same time? How do you decide how big a priority you want to make debt repayment?

Personal Dreamstorm

❖ What are three things you want to see (or support) in the national budget?

Budget Action Plan

❖ Based on the three things you want to see (or support) in the national budget, what is one thing you could do now to move toward making them a reality?

❖ What is some information you need or connections you could make to help you? (See resources below for ideas if you need them.)

❖ List three action steps you will take in the next six months, listing the step, with whom, and a timeline.

National Debt Questions

If you pay taxes, you pay about $1,468 each year to interest on the national debt (this amount varies from state to state — this is the figure for Illinois).

❖ How do you feel about this?

❖ Are there some things you are willing to pay interest on the debt for? What are they?

❖ Are there some things you don't want to pay interest on the debt for? What are they?

❖ We had a surplus a few years ago in the national budget. What would you have spent that surplus on?

Personal Income and Tax Analysis

❖ Do you feel you pay too many taxes? If so, why?

❖ Do you think some people should pay less or some people should pay more?

❖ Would you be willing to pay more if you felt that the programs your taxes were used for benefited people in your community who had fewer resources than you or provided community programs that are needed by all?

Resources for Taking Action

This is not a comprehensive list but a jumping-off place. Refer also to the "Sources" section of this book for more resources and background information. If you know of any other good resources, let me know — send an e-mail from my website <www.womenandtheus budget.com>.

The resources listed below are organized according to the guiding principles for a new budget from Chapter 8.

1. Commitment to meet the basic human needs of all people for food, housing, healthcare, education, protection from violence, jobs at good wages, and adequate social safety nets for those who can't work.

AFL-CIO
815 16th Street NW
Washington, DC 20006
(202) 637-5000
Fax (202) 637-5058
www.aflcio.org

Campaign for America's Future
1025 Connecticut Avenue NW
Suite 205
Washington, DC 20036
(202) 955-5665
Fax (202) 955-5606
www.ourfuture.org

Campaign for a National Health
Program NOW!
339 Lafayette Street
New York, NY 10012-2725
(212) 475-8350
(800) 453-1305
www.cnhpnow.org

Coalition on Human Needs
1120 Connecticut Avenue NW
Suite 910
Washington, DC 20036

(202) 223-2532 x 29
Fax (202) 223-2538
jbeeson@chn.org
www.chn.org

Economic Policy Institute (EPI)
1660 L Street NW, Suite 1200
Washington, DC 20036
(202) 775-8810
Fax (202) 775-0819
epi@epinet.
www.epinet.org

Families USA
1334 G Street NW
Washington, DC 20005
(202) 628-3030
Fax (202) 347-2417
info@familiesusa.org

Food Research and Action
Center
1875 Connecticut Avenue NW
Suite 540
Washington, DC 20009
(202) 986-2200
Fax (202) 986-2525

webmaster@frac.org
www.frac.org

Good Jobs First
1311 L Street NW
Washington, DC 20005
(202) 626-3780
Fax (202) 638-3486
info@goodjobsfirst.org
www.goodjobsfirst.org

National Low Income Housing
Coalition (NLIHC)
1012 Fourteenth Street NW
Suite 610
Washington, DC 20005
(202) 662-1530
Fax (202) 393-1973
info@nlihc.org
www.nlihc.org/

National Priorities Project
17 New South Street, Suite 302
Northampton, MA 01060
(413) 584-9556
Fax (413) 58-9647
info@nationalpriorities.org
www.nationalpriorities.org

National Welfare Rights Union
4750 Woodward Avenue
Suite 402
Detroit, MI 48201
(313) 832-0618
Fax (313) 832-1409
info@nationalwru.org
www.nationalwru.org

UNITE HERE Headquarters
(formerly the Union of
Needletrades, Textiles and
Industrial Employees and the
Hotel Employees and Restaurant
Employees International Union)
275 7th Avenue
New York, NY 10001-6708
(212) 265-7000
info@behindthelabel.org
www.unitehere.org

Urban Institute
2100 M Street NW
Washington, DC 20037
(202) 833-7200
paffairs@ui.urban.org
www.urban.org

2. Equitable distribution of the nation's resources, income, and wealth.

Center on Budget and Policy
Priorities (CBPP)
International Budget Network
820 1st Street NE, Suite 510
Washington, DC 20002
(202) 408-1080
Fax (202) 408-1056
center@cbpp.org
www.cbpp.org/

Citizens for Tax Justice (CTJ)
1311 L Street NW
Washington, DC 20005
(202) 626-3780
Fax (202) 638-3486
www.ctj.org

Dollars & Sense
The Magazine of Economic

Justice
740 Cambridge Street
Cambridge, MA 02141
(617) 876-2434
Fax (617) 876-0008
dollars@dollarsandsense.org
www.dollarsandsense.org

International Association For
Feminist Economics (IAFFE)
PO Box 9430
Richmond, VA 23228
Fax (313) 731-0174
clsmith@iaffe.org
www.iaffe.org

Union of Radical Political
Economists (URPE)
Gordon Hall, University

of Massachusetts
418 North Pleasant Street
Amherst, MA 01002-1735
(413) 577-0806
urpe@labornet.org

United for a Fair Economy
37 Temple Place, 2nd Floor
Boston, MA 02111
(617) 423-2148
Fax (617) 423-0191
info@faireconomy.org
www.faireconomy.org

3. Financial self-sufficiency for women and people of color, as well as the full development of young people.

Center for the Advancement
of Women
25 West 43 Street, Suite 1120
New York, NY 10036
(212) 391-7718
info@advancewomen.org
www.advancewomen.org

Center for Policy Alternatives
1875 Connecticut Avenue NW
Suite 710
Washington, DC 20009
(202) 387-6030
Fax (202) 387-8529
www.cfpa.org

Children's Defense Fund
25 E Street NW
Washington, DC 20001
(202) 628-8787
cdfinfo@childrensdefense.org
www.childrensdefense.org

Church Women United
The Interchurch Center
475 Riverside Drive, Suite 1626
New York, NY 10115
(212) 870-2347
(800) 298-5551
Fax (212) 870-2338
cwu@churchwomen.org
www.churchwomen.org

Feminist Majority Foundation
1600 Wilson Boulevard
Suite 801
Arlington, VA 22209
(703) 522-2214

Fax (703) 522-2219
www.feminist.org

Institute for Women's
Policy Research
1707 L Street NW, Suite 750
Washington, DC 20036
(202) 785-5100
Fax (202) 833-4362
iwpr@iwpr.org
www.iwpr.org

National Committee on
Pay Equity
1925 K Street NW, Suite 402
Washington, DC 20006-1119
(202) 223-8360, Ext. 8
Fax (202) 776-0537
fairpay@pay-equity.org
www.pay-equity.org

National Organization for
Women (NOW)
1100 H Street NW, 3rd Floor
Washington, DC 20005
(202) 628-8669
Fax (202) 785-8576
now@now.org
www.now.org

United Methodist
Women's Division
General Board of
Global Ministries
United Methodist Church
475 Riverside Drive
New York, NY 101151
(800) 862-4246
http://gbgm-umc.org/umw

United Nations Commission
on the Status of Women
2 UN Plaza, DC2-12th Floor
New York, NY 10017
Fax (212) 963-3463
daw@un.org
www.un.org/womenwatch/daw

UNIFEM Headquarters in New
York
United Nations Development
Fund for Women
304 East 45 Street, 15th Floor
New York, NY 10017
(212) 906-6400
Fax (212) 906-6705

Wider Opportunities for Women
1001 Connecticut Avenue NW,
Suite 930
Washington, DC 20036
(202) 464-1596

Fax (202) 464-1660
info@WOWonline.org.
www.wowonline.org

Women's Economic Agenda
Project
Women and Family Center
449 15th Street, 2nd Floor
Oakland, CA 94612
(510) 451-7379
Fax (510) 986-8628
weap@weap.org
www.weap.org

Women's International Coalition
for Economic Justice (WICEJ)
12 Dorgan Place, Suite 206
New York, NY 10040
(212) 304-9106
Fax (646) 349-2195
info@wicej.org
www.wicej.org

4. Peace-directed foreign policy, with an emphasis on working within multilateral institutions such as United Nations bodies and agencies, and the International Criminal Court.

American Friends Service
Committee
1501 Cherry Street
Philadelphia, PA 19102
(215) 241-7000
Fax (215) 241-7275
afscinfo@afsc.org
www.afsc.org

United for Peace and Justice
PO Box 607
Times Square Station
New York, NY 10108
(212) 868-5545
www.unitedforpeace.org

Win Without War
(202) 822-2075
www.winwithoutwarus.org

Women's Action for New
Directions (WAND)
691 Massachusetts Avenue

Arlington, MA 02476
(781) 643-6740
Fax (781) 643-6744
info@wand.org
www.wand.org

Women's Edge Coalition
1825 Connecticut Avenue NW,
Suite 800
Washington, DC 20009
(202) 884-8396
edge@womensedge.org
www.womensedge.org/index.jsp

Women's International League
for Peace and Freedom (WILPF)
US National Office
1213 Race Street
Philadelphia, PA 19107
(215) 563-7110
wilpf@wilpf.org
www.wilpf.org

5. Public life and discourse that are democratic, welcome diversity, and dismantle discrimination based on race, ethnicity, gender, age, class, ability, and sexual orientation.

Applied Research Center
3781 Broadway
Oakland, CA 94611
(510) 653-3415
Fax (510) 653-3427
www.arc.org

Association for White Anti-
Racist Education (AWARE)
PO Box 1372
Brentwood, TN 37024-1372
(615) 463-2689
warn@home.com

Center for Public Integrity
910 17th Street NW, Suite 700
Washington, DC 20006
(202) 466-1300
www.publicintegrity.org/

Center for Third World
Organizing
1218 East 21st Street
Oakland, CA 94606
(510) 533-7583
Fax (510) 533-0923
ctwo@ctwo.org
www.ctwo.org

Coalition of the Moving Ideas
Network
2000 L Street NW, Suite 717
Washington, DC 20036
(202) 776-0730
Fax (202) 776-0740
movingideas@movingideas.org

Colorado Women's Agenda
400 Corona Avenue, Suite B
Denver, CO 80218
(303) 863-7336
Fax (303) 830-1502

Fair Vote — Center for Voting
and Democracy
6930 Carroll Avenue, Suite 610
Takoma Park, MD 20912

(301) 270-4616
www.fairvote.org

50 Years is Enough Network
3628 12th Street NE
Washington, DC 20017
(202) 463-2265
info@50years.org
www.50years.org

Indigenous Women's Network
Alma de Miyer
13621 FM 2769
Austin, TX 78726
(512) 258-3880
Fax (512) 258-1858
info@indigenouswomen.org
www.indigenouswomen.org

National Association for
Commissions of Women
(NACW)
8630 Fenton Street, Suite 934
Silver Spring, MD 20910
(301) 585-8101
Fax (301) 585-3445
nacw@nacw.org
www.nacw.org

National Coalition of Blacks for
Reparations in America
(N'COBRA)
PO Box 90604
Washington, DC 20090-0604
(202) 291-8400
Fax (202) 291-4600
www.ncobra.com

National Voice
2105 First Avenue South
Minneapolis, MN 55404
(612) 879-7500
(866) 428-7228
www.nationalvoice.org

Office of the High
Commissioner for Human

Rights
8-14 Avenue de la Paix
1211 Geneva 10
Switzerland
(41-22) 917-9000
Fax (41-22) 917-9016
www.unhchr.ch

The People's Institute for
Survival and Beyond
1444 North Johnson
New Orleans, LA 70116
(504) 944-2354
www.thepeoplesinstitute.org

Program on Corporations, Law
and Democracy (POCLAD)

PO Box 246
S. Yarmouth, MA 02664-0246
(508) 398-1145
Fax (508) 398-1552
people@poclad.org
www.poclad.org

Women of Color Resource
Center
1611 Telegraph Avenue,
Suite 303
Oakland, CA 94612
(510) 444-2700
Fax (510) 444-2711
info@coloredgirls.org
www.coloredgirls.org

6. Support of the variety of economic, cultural, spiritual, and artistic
   expression of communities.

Action Without Borders
360 West 31st Street, Suite 1510
New York, NY 10001
(212) 843-3973
Fax (212) 564-3377
info@idealist.org
www.idealist.org

Art for the World
28 rue de l'Athenée
Clt-1206 Geneva
Switzerland
(41-22) 789 15 55
infor@artfortheworld.net
www.artfortheworld.net

Art in the Public Interest
PO Box 68
Saxapanaw, NC 27340
(336) 376-8404
www.apionline.org

Bread and Puppet Theater
Rd #2
Glover, VT 05839
(802) 525-3031
breadpup@together.net
www.theaterofmemory.com/art/
bread/bread.html

Institute for Local Self-Reliance
927 15th Street NW, 4th Floor
Washington, DC 20005
(202) 898-1610
www.ilsr.org

Spirit in Action
274 North Street
Belchertown, MA 01007
(413) 256-4612
Fax (413) 256-4613
info@spiritinaction.net
www.spiritinaction.net

7. Harmony with ecological processes and sustainability of natural
   resources.

EnviroLink Network
PO Box 8102
Pittsburgh, PA 15217
www.envirolink.org/

Friends of the Earth
1717 Massachusetts Avenue
NW, Suite 600
Washington, DC 20036-2002

(877) 843-8687
Fax (202) 783-0444
foe@foe.org
www.foe.org

Southwest Research and
Information Center
105 Stanford SE
PO Box 4524
Albuquerque, NM 87106
(505) 262-1862
Fax (505) 262-1864
Info@sric.org.

White Earth Land Recovery
Project
32033 East Round Lake Road
Ponsford, MN 56575
(218) 573-3448
(888) 779-3577
Fax (218) 573-3444
www.welrp.org

Women's Environment &
Development Organization
(WEDO)
355 Lexington Avenue,
3rd Floor
New York, NY 10017

(212) 973-0325
Fax (212) 973-0335
www.wedo.org

US Government Resources
US Department of Labor
Women's Bureau
Frances Perkins Building
200 Constitution Avenue NW
Washington, DC 20210
(800) 827-5335
www.dol.gov/wb/

United States Office of
the Treasury
Office of Tax Policy
www.treas.gov/offices/tax-policy/

Assistant Secretary (Tax Policy)
Department of the Treasury
1500 Pennsylvania Avenue NW,
Room 3120
Washington, DC 20220
General Information:
(202) 622-2000

A gateway to federal statistics:
www.fedstats.gov/key_stats/
BEAkey.html

WOMEN'S COMMISSIONS

President John F. Kennedy established the President's Commission on the Status of Women in 1961. Eleanor Roosevelt was the chair and Esther Peterson of the US Department of Labor's Women's Bureau was vice-chair. Now there are approximately 270 state, county, and local commissions for women in the United States and its territories.

Commissions advocate for equality and justice for women and serve their communities in a variety of ways. Many maintain shelters for women who have experienced domestic violence, while others run programs for teens and adults, testify before legislators on issues that affect women and their families, and disseminate information to their constituency. The National Association for Commissions of Women (NACW) provides national leadership and focuses the collective concerns of the commissions. (Visit the NACW website < www.nacw.org> for more information and to find out if there is a commission in your community.)

Notes

❖

Chapter 1

1. Sue Tucker speaking at "The Money Game in Time of War," a panel presentation put on by the Women's Action for New Directions (WAND) Education Fund, December 11, 2001.

Chapter 3

1. Diane Dujon speaking at a panel presentation on human needs budget cuts, Massachusetts state capitol, Boston, MA, July 1996.

2. Connecticut Attorney General's Office. "Attorney General Files Suit Against Bristol-Myers Squibb for Anti-Trust Violations" [online]. [Cited March 22, 2005]. Press release, June 4, 2002. <www.cslib.org/attygenl/press/2002/coniss/taxol.htm>.

3. Government Accountability Office. "Financial Management: Further Actions Are Needed to Establish Framework to Guide Audit Opinion and Business Management Improvement Efforts at DOD." GAO-04-910R. GAO, September 20, 2004.

4. Brian Awehali. "David and Goliath in Indian Country" [online]. [Cited August 10, 2004]. Article posted on AlterNet, October 27, 2003.<www.alternet.org/story/17026>.

5. Daniel Pulliam. "Notification of Sale" [online]. [Cited October 10, 2004]. Article posted on GovExec.com, October 8, 2004. <www.govexec.com/dailyfed/ 0904/100804lb.htm>.

Chapter 4

1. William Greider. "The End of Empire" [online]. [Cited March 22. 2005]. Article in The Nation, September 5, 2002. <www.thenation.com/doc.mhtml?i=20020923&s=greider>.

2. Andrew Ferguson. "Bush Harks Back to Reagan's Legacy of Deficits" [online]. [Cited October 10, 2004]. Article in Los Angeles Business Journal, February 10, 2003. <www.labusinessjournal.com>.

Chapter 5

1. Quoted in Eric Pashnik. "Budgeting More, Deciding Less: Budget Politics and Social Policy." Public Interest. Winter 2000. Available online <www. findarticles.com/p/articles/mi_m0377/is_2000_Wntr/ai_58672901>.

2. Congressional Quarterly. Powers of Congress. Congressional Quarterly Press, 1982, p. 13.

3. Joint Committee on the Reorganization of Congress. "Organization of the Congress" [online]. [Cited June 10, 2004]. Final report, December 1993. <www. house.gov/rules/jcoc2c.htm>.

4. Robert Longley. "Government Shutdown?" [online]. [Cited September 13, 2004]. Article posted on about.com, October 24, 1999. <http://usgovinfo. about.com/library/weekly/aa102499p2.htm>.

5. House Judiciary Committee Democratic Staff. "Preserving Democracy: What Went Wrong in Ohio?" [online]. [Cited March 15, 2004]. Report issued January 5, 2005. <www.nvri.org/about/ohio_conyers_report_010505.pdf>.

6. Sean Loughlin and Robert Yoon. "Millionaires Populate US Senate" [online]. [Cited December 10, 2004]. Article posted on CNN website, June 13, 2003. <www.cnn.com/2003/ALLPOLITICS/06/13/senators.finances/>.

7. Azza Karam and Joni Lovenduski. "Learning the Rules" [online]. [Cited November 15, 2004]. Section of chapter "Women in Politics: Making a Difference" in Women in Politics: Beyond Numbers on the International IDEA (Institute for Democracy and Electoral Assistance) website, June 1998. <archive.idea.int/women/parl/ch5c.htm>.

Chapter 6

1. Richard Grossman and Frank T. Adams. "Taking Care of Business." Conscious Choice. January 1996. Available online <www.consciouschoice.com/1995-98/cc091/takingcareofbusiness.html>.

2. William Greider. One World Ready or Not: The Manic Logic of Global Capitalism. Simon & Schuster, 1998, p. 24.

3. Representative Wright Patman (D-TX). "The A B C's Of America's Money System." Congressional Record, 88th Cong., 2nd sess., August 3, 1964.

Chapter 7

1. Kofi Annan. "Transcript of Press Conference by Secretary-General Kofi Annan on Financing for Development at Headquarters" [online]. [Cited March 23, 2004]. United Nations Information Service, December 18, 2000. <www.unis. unvienna.org/unis/ pressrels/2000/sg2750.html>.

2. Peggy Antrobus, quoted in Zonny Woods. "IMF and World Bank Structural Adjustment Programs and Their Effects on Women" [online]. [Cited November 10, 2004]. Youth Sourcebook on Sustainable Development, International Institute for Sustainable Development, 1995. <http://iisd.ca/youth/ysbk077.htm>.

3. Steve Lohr. "An Elder Challenges Outsourcing's Orthodoxy." New York Times. September 9, 2004. Available online <http://scid.stanford.edu/ publications/InTheNews/tnsrinivasan090904.pdf>.

4. Jubilee 2000. "Bolivian Civil Society Asserts Demand For Involvement In Fight For Debt Cancellation And Poverty Reduction" [online]. [Cited November 15, 2004]. <www.jubilee2000uk.org/ jubilee2000/news/bolivia1 60500.html>.

5. Jim Lobe. " Sharp Increase in U.S. Military Aid to Latin America" [online]. [Cited March 23, 2004]. Article at Common Dreams News Center, September 23, 2003. <www.commondreams.org/ headlines03/0923-02.htm>.

6. Michael Switow. "Malaysia Mahatir Vs. 'Immoral' Markets" [online]. [Cited December 11, 2004]. Article in the Christian Science Monitor, September 24, 1997. <http://csmonitor.com/cgibin/durableRedirect.pl?/durable/1997/09/24/econ/econ.1.html>.

7. UNIFEM. "Conference Urges Governments, Multilateral Agencies, NGOs to Incorporate Gender Analysis in National Budgets" [online]. [Cited September 20, 2004]. Press release, October 18, 2001. <www.unifem.org/press releases.php?f_page_pid=6&f_pritem_pid=52>.

Chapter 8

1. The Women's Budget Project held a joint training session with the Massachusetts Women's Economic Agenda Project on July 18, 1997, at Boston City Hall. Attending were Kelly Bates, Marie Turley, Becky Johnson, Loretta Williams, George Friday, Gillian Gilhool, Laura Russell, Maya Hasegawa, Grove Harris, Lisa McGowan, Joanie Cohen, Marian Chatfield-Taylor, Ann Griffiths, Jane Midgley, Jean Kluver, Joan Miller, Elena Swain.

2. The Women's Budget Project held a national meeting from October 18 to 20, 1996, in Philadelphia, PA, at the headquarters of the Women's International League for Peace and Freedom (WILPF). Those in attendance were Marion Anderson, Employment Research Associates; Carol Barton, popular economics educator; Alisha Berry, student organizer; Marilyn Clement, WILPF; Jeanne Guanna, Southwest Organizing Committee; L.J. Hopkins, United Methodist, Women's Division; Jennifer Jackman, Feminist Majority Foundation; Marian Kramer, National Welfare Rights Union; Eleanor LeCain, Women's Action for New Directions; Ethel Longscott, Women's Economic Agenda Project; Miriam Louie, Women of Color Resource Center; Jane Midgley, Women's Budget Project; elmira nzombe, National Council of Churches; Denise O'Brien, National Family Farm Coalition; Robin Randle,

Federation of Southern Co-ops; Edie Rasell, Economic Policy Institute; Martha Reumann, Evangelical Lutheran Church; and Agnes Williams, Indigenous Women's Network (organizational affiliations are those of participants in 1996). Arlene Allen facilitated. Pam Sparr was instrumental in organizing the meeting.

GLOSSARY

Allocations: In the budget resolution, limits on the amount of money available for discretionary spending, which are given to appropriations and authorization committees as spending ceilings.

Appropriation: An act of Congress that provides the legal authority for federal agencies to make payments for specific things (i.e., programs or administration). Appropriations must be passed by both the House and the Senate and signed by the president to become law.

Appropriations committees: Committees in the House and Senate that decide on the annual spending in 13 areas of federal discretionary spending. Appropriations committees send their recommendations to the full Senate and House for further deliberation and eventual passage of 13 appropriations bills.

Authorization: An act of Congress that establishes, changes, or continues the operation of a federal agency or program. Authorizing legislation is normally a prerequisite for appropriations. For some programs, mainly entitlements, the authorizing legislation itself provides the authority to incur obligations and make payments. Like appropriations acts, authorizing legislation must be passed by both houses of Congress and signed by the president to become law.

Authorization committees: Committees in the House and Senate that decide which agencies and programs will be granted the right to receive funding. Authorization committees have jurisdiction over mandatory spending in the federal budget process.

Bond: A certificate that promises repayment of a debt. Bonds can be issued by the government or by a company; the issuer agrees to pay back the borrowed money at a fixed rate of interest on a specified date.

Budget: A forecast of expenditures and revenues for a specific period of time that is used to set priorities as well as monitor progress towards goals.

Budget authority: The authority to make commitments that will result in immediate or future spending of federal funds (everything except trust funds). Budget authority sets the amount of new commitments that can be made. It is not the same as actual spending in a given year, which is known as outlays.

Budget committees: Committees — one in the House and one in the Senate, created under the Congressional Budget and Impoundment Control Act of 1974 — that are responsible for preparing budget resolutions for each budget cycle and reconciling differences between House and Senate versions of the budget.

Budget functions: The categories used to organize the president's budget proposal. The functions group all federal programs according to their purpose.

Budget of the United States Government: Documents issued by the Office of Management and Budget each February that include the president's budget proposals, supporting documents, charts, analyses, and historical records of budgets passed.

Budget reconciliation: A legislative process Congress uses to ensure taxes and spending proposals conform with the targets set out in the budget resolution — that is, to reconcile tax and spending legislation with the budget. The reconciliation process primarily affects taxes, entitlement spending, and offsetting receipts. As a rule, decisions on discretionary programs are determined separately through the appropriations process.

Budget resolution: The budget resolution sets targets for spending, including the upper limit of what can be spent in broad program areas. Known as the Concurrent Budget Resolution, it must be passed in identical form by both the House and Senate each year, setting forth a congressional budget plan. The resolution does not require the president's signature and does not become law. To be implemented, its directives must be carried out through subsequent legislation, including appropriations and changes in tax and entitlement laws.

Capital budget: A plan for capital expenditure (i.e., for investment in long-term assets such as buildings, plant, and equipment and in multi-year physical and ongoing projects such as infrastructure improvement). A capital budget does not include money spent for present needs and current consumption.

Care economy: The care economy produces family and community-oriented goods and services as part of the process of caring for people. Workers in the care economy are not paid, though they may be supported by transfer payments from the government (such as pensions and child benefits).

Conference committee: A conference committee is a temporary panel of House and Senate negotiators. It is created to resolve differences between versions of similar House and Senate bills, including those pertaining to the budget.

Congressional Budget Office (CBO): A nonpartisan office serving Congress. CBO's role is to provide independent, objective, technical economic and budgetary information to Congress. CBO was created by the Congressional Budget Act of 1974 to free Congress from relying on the administration's Office of Management and Budget (OMB) for budgetary and economic information.

Contingent workers: Part-time and/or temporary workers who perform services, often on a contract basis, that were previously performed in-house. These flexible arrangements, along with other arrangements that do not involve workers with full-time wages and salaries, have come to be referred to as "contingent work" by labor market analysts.

Continuing resolution: An appropriations act intended to continue funding for certain programs when the normal appropriations legislation for those programs has not been enacted by the start of the fiscal year. Also known as a "CR," it provides temporary funding, normally at current levels or less.

Corporate income taxes: Provisions in the US tax code that regulate the amount and form of taxes corporations owe to the US government.

Corporate profits: Profit, in business, is the monetary difference between the cost of producing and marketing goods or services, and the price subsequently received for those goods or services. The will to make and function by profits is termed the profit motive.

Custom duties: The money collected from tariffs is called a customs duty. A tariff is a tax levied by a government on imports and exports. Although tariffs are a source of government revenue, they are also used to carry out political and economic policies in the international economy.

Debt ceiling: The amount that the country is allowed to go into debt. The debt ceiling is set in legislation passed by Congress and signed by the president, usually annually. Congress must enact new legislation to raise the ceiling.

Debt held by the public: The part of the gross federal debt owed to people and institutions outside the government.

Deficit: The result when spending exceeds income in the annual budget.

Depression: In economics, a period in an industrial nation characterized by low production and sales and high rates of business failures and unemployment.

Discretionary spending: Spending that the president and Congress decide through passage of 13 appropriations bills annually. This spending is optional each year, in contrast to entitlement programs for which funding is mandatory.

Entitlements: Programs that legally obligate the federal government to make payments to any person who meets the legal criteria for eligibility, such as Social Security, Medicare, and Medicaid.

Excise taxes: Taxes imposed on the sale of specific goods or services, or on licenses to engage in certain activities. Excise taxes, also called selective sales taxes, are considered consumption taxes because they raise the prices of certain commodities for consumers, such as alcohol, tobacco, transportation fuels, and telephone service.

Federal Insurance Contributions Act (FICA): Two titles of the Social Security Act specified the manner in which taxes would be deducted from workers' earnings to finance both old-age benefits and unemployment compensation. These tax laws were later written into the code of the Internal Revenue Service. The Social Security tax became known by the name of one of these laws, the Federal Insurance Contributions Act (FICA).

Federal poverty measure: The standard used by the US government to classify people as "poor." There are two versions: poverty thresholds and poverty guidelines. Thresholds are standards issued annually by the Census Bureau for estimating the number of people living in poverty. Guidelines are standards issued by the Department of Health and Human Services for measuring eligibility for certain federal programs.

Federal Reserve banks: Banks that are part of the Federal Reserve system (the "Fed"). Most of the Fed's day-to-day operations are left to the officers of 12 district Federal Reserve banks, located throughout the nation. Most commercial banks are also members of the Fed.

Federal Reserve system: The "Fed," as it is known, was established by the Federal Reserve Act of 1913 as a way to create a stable banking system and monetary policy for the country. The act mandated the creation of a central banking system divided into regional Federal Reserve banks.

Federal trust funds: Government accounts, established by law as trust funds, that collect and spend revenues for specific purposes, such as the Social Security trust funds.

GDP: GDP stands for gross domestic product, which is a measure of the total value of goods and services produced within a country over a specified time period, normally a year. Income arising from investments abroad is not included.

Globalization: The growing economic, political, technological, and cultural linkages that connect individuals, communities, businesses, and governments around the world. Globalization also involves the growth of multinational corporations (businesses that have operations or investments in many countries) and transnational corporations (businesses that see themselves functioning in a global marketplace). The international institutions that oversee world trade and finance (i.e., the World Trade Organization, the World Bank, and the International Monetary Fund) play an increasingly important role in this era of globalization.

GNP: GNP stands for gross national product, which is a measure of the value of the goods and services produced by the residents of a country, regardless of where the assets are located, over a specified time period, normally a year. It includes income from US investments abroad.

Government Accountability Office (GAO): The office in Congress that audits federal agencies and programs. (This used to be the Government Accounting Office — the name was changed in July 2004.)

Gross federal debt: The total amount of money the government has borrowed over time that still has to be repaid.

Individual income taxes: Provisions in the US tax code that regulate the amount and form of taxes that individuals owe the US government.

Intragovernmental holdings: The amount of the gross federal debt the government owes to the federal trust funds. (The trust funds are required to lend any trust fund excess to the government.)

Macroeconomics: The study of the behavior of the economy as a whole, focusing on variables such as employment, inflation, growth, and stability.

Mandatory spending: Spending that is not controlled by annual decisions of Congress. The government is automatically obligated to spend this money because of previously enacted laws. Mandatory spending programs are also known as entitlements.

Microeconomics: The study of individual decision making in response to changes in prices and incomes.

Monetary Policy: Economic principles and programs adopted by a government that manage the growth of its money supply, the availability of credit, and interest rates. In the United States, the Federal Reserve Board determines monetary policy.

National Debt: Known in the official budget as the gross federal debt, this is the accumulation of deficits, minus any surpluses.

National wealth: The total monetary value of all the capital and goods owned by a particular country at any given time.

North American Free Trade Agreement (NAFTA): A pact that calls for the gradual removal of tariffs and other trade barriers on most goods produced and sold in North America. NAFTA became effective in Canada, Mexico, and the United States on January 1, 1994. It forms the world's second largest free-trade zone, bringing together 365 million consumers in the three countries in an open market.

Off-budget: Describes programs not counted towards budget limits due to provisions in current law. For example, Social Security trust funds and the postal service are currently off-budget programs. (If the law changes and these programs are counted towards the budget, they are "on-budget.")

Office of Management and Budget (OMB): A federal agency that prepares the president's budget submission to Congress and provides him with economic forecasts. OMB serves the president and acts as an advocate for the president's policies.

Omnibus bill: An omnibus bill packages several measures together in one bill or combines diverse subjects into a single bill. Examples are reconciliation bills and combined appropriations bills.

Open market operations: The Federal Reserve's principal tool for implementing monetary policy, open market operations involve the purchase and sale of US Treasury bonds and federal agency securities, which changes the supply of reserves and the circulation of money throughout the system. The Fed buys bonds when it wants to lower interest rates, and sells bonds when it wants to raise interest rates.

Outlays: The amount of money actually spent by the government in a given year. This may include current budget authority and unexpended budget authority from past years. Also known as expenditures.

Recession: In economics, a decline in economic activity, a period, shorter than a depression, during which there is a decline in economic trade and prosperity.

Savings bond: A registered bond issued by the US government in denominations of $50 to $10,000. Savings bonds yield maximum interest when they mature after a considerable number of years.

Structural adjustment programs (SAPs): Structural adjustment programs are conditions that the International Monetary Fund sets that developing countries must agree to if they want access to loans from international trade institutions. Measures that developing countries have had to take under SAPs include devaluing currency, reducing wages, privatizing state-owned industries, cutting social service employment, and cutting social spending.

System of National Accounts (SNA): A coherent, consistent, and integrated set of macroeconomic accounts, balance sheets, and tables based on a set of internationally agreed concepts, definitions, classifications, and accounting rules. It is used to calculate GDP.

Tax code: The collection of laws that guide the way taxes are assessed and collected. It includes things such as the rates at which people and corporations must pay different taxes and when and how the taxes must be paid. It consists of many parts and is 7 million words and thousands of pages.

Tax expenditure: Revenue that does not come to the federal government because of provisions in the tax laws that allow a special exclusion, exemption, or deduction from gross income or that allow a special credit, a preferential rate of tax, or a deferral of tax liability.

Underemployed: Employed persons who have expressed the desire to work additional hours in their present job or in an additional job, or to take a new job with longer working hours.

Veto: The procedure established under the Constitution by which the president refuses to approve a bill or joint resolution (including budget-related legislation) and thus prevents its enactment into law. The president usually returns a vetoed bill with a message indicating his reasons for rejecting the measure. The veto can be overridden only by a two-thirds vote in both the Senate and the House.

Working poor: Individuals who spend at least 27 weeks a year in the labor force (working or looking for work), but whose incomes fall below the official poverty level.

World Trade Organization (WTO): Established in 1994, the World Trade Organization (WTO) took over the activities of the General Agreement on Tariffs and Trade (GATT). The WTO's system focuses on corporate-managed trade, economic efficiency, and short-run corporate profits.

Sources

❖

Chapter 1

AFL-CIO. "Pay Gap Between Women and Men: Same as in 1983" [online]. [Cited October 30,2004]. Press release, December 4, 2003. www.aflcio.org /issuespolitics/women/equalpay/ns1 2042003.cfm.

AFL-CIO. "The New Medicare Bill at a Glance" [online]. [Cited October 20, 2004]. Fact sheet, n.d. <www.aflcio.org/issuespolitics/medicare/new_bill.cfm>.

Amott, Teresa L. "Wealth and Its Distribution." In *Reader's Companion to U.S. Women's History.* Houghton Mifflin, 1998. Available online <http://college.hmco. com/ history/ readerscomp/women/html/wh_038900_wealthandits.htm>.

Amott, Teresa L., and Julie Matthaei. *Race, Gender and Work: A Multi-Cultural Economic History of Women in the United States.* South End Press, 1996.

Anderson, Darah, and John Cavanagh. "World's Billionaires Take a Hit, But Still Soar" [online]. [Cited November 15, 2004]. Article on Institute for Policy Studies website, March 6, 2002. <www.ips-dc.org/projects/global_econ/ billionaires.htm>.

Berkowitz, Bill. "Prospecting Among the Poor: Welfare Privatization" [online]. [Cited November 5, 2004]. Report for Applied Research Center, May 2001. <www.arc.org/ downloads/ prospecting.pdf>.

Bernhardt, Annette, Laura Dresser, and Catherine Hill. "Why Privatizing Government Services Would Hurt Women Workers" [online]. [Cited September 4, 2004]. Report for the Institute for Women's Policy Research, October 2003. <www.iwpr.org/pdf/ Privatizing%20Govt%2010-00.pdf>.

Business and Professional Women's Foundation. "Workingwomen Speak Out Survey" [online]. [Cited September 4, 2004]. Report on survey, August 2004. <www. bpwusa.org/content/PressRoom/WorkingwomenSpeakOut/ workingwomensurvey.htm>.

CBS News. "Bush's 2nd Term Poll — Part 2" [online]. [Cited March 18, 2005].

CBS/<I>New York Times<i> poll, January 19, 2005. <www.cbsnews.com/stories/2005/01/19/opinion/polls/main667938.shtml>.

Center for Labor Market Studies. "Treading Water in Quicksand: A Look at Poverty, Income Inadequacy and Self-Sufficiency in Massachusetts" [online]. [Cited March 18, 2005]. Prepared for the Workforce Solutions Group using the Women's Educational and Industrial Union's Self-Sufficiency Standard, September 2004. <www.weiu.org/Advocacy/Treading_Water.pdf>.

Families USA. "Going without Health Insurance: One in Three Non-Elderly Americans, 2002–2003" [online]. [Cited October 10, 2004]. Report from Families USA, June 2003. <www.familiesusa.org/site/DocServer/82million_uninsured_report.pdf? docID=3641>.

Government Accountability Office. "Women's Earnings: Work Patterns Partially Explain Difference between Men's and Women's Earnings." GAO-04-35. GAO. October 2003. Available online <www.gao.gov/new.items/d0435.pdf>.

Hartmann, Heidi. "Women's Earnings Fall: U.S. Census Bureau Finds Rising Gender Wage Gap." Press release from the Institute for Women's Policy Research, August 27, 2004, p. 1.

Hartmann, Heidi I., and Stephen J. Rose. "Still a Man's Labor Market: The Long-Term Earnings Gap" [online]. [Cited November 20, 2004]. Report for the Institute for Women's Policy Research, June 2004. <www.iwpr.org/pdf/C355.pdf>.

Joint Center for Political and Economic Studies. "Income and Poverty Among African Americans" [online]. [Cited March 18, 2005]. DataBank brief, 2004, pp. 7–8. <www.jointcenter.org/ 2004election/CBC-health-briefs/Economic+Brief.pdf>.

Kochhar, Rakesh. "The Wealth of Hispanic Households" [online]. [Cited December 10, 2004]. Report for the Pew Hispanic Center, October 18, 2004. <http://pewhispanic.org/reports/report.php? ReportID=34>.

Krugman, Paul. "Borrow, Speculate and Hope." *New York Times*. December 10, 2004.

Long Scott, Ethel. "Health Care: An Economic Human Right; Building a Broad Social Movement for Health Care as a Human Right" [online]. [Cited November 10, 2004]. Presentation for Women's Economic Agenda Project, 2004. <www.weap. org/ 60million/60million.html>.

Midgley, Jane. "Privatization Threatens Social Security." *Peace and Freedom* (Women's International League for Peace and Freedom). March/April 1998, pp. 22–23.

Rother, Larry. "Chile's Retirees Find Shortfall in Private Plan." *New York Times*. January 27, 2005, p. 1.

Social Security Administration. "Social Security Is Important to Women" [online]. [Cited March 19, 2005]. Fact sheet, September 2004. <www.social security.gov/pressoffice/factsheets/women.htm>.

US Department of Labor, Employee Benefits Security Administration. "Women and Retirement Savings" [online]. [Cited November 15, 2004]. Fact sheet., n.d. <www. dol.gov/ebsa/publications/women.html>.

Women's Educational and Industrial Union in collaboration with Wider Opportunities for Women. "The Self-Sufficiency Standard: Where Massachusetts Families Stand" [online]. [Cited March 23, 2005]. Report prepared for the Massachusetts Family Economic Self-Sufficiency Project, January 2000. <www.weiu. org/pdf_files/WMFSFinalVersion.pdf>.

"Women Who Early In Life Care For Elderly Parents Are More Likely To Be Economically Disadvantaged In Later Years" [online]. [Cited March 23, 2004]. Press release from Rice University, August 16, 2004. <www.media. rice.edu/media/NewsBot.asp?MODE=VIEW&ID=4912&SnID=388481692>.

Chapter 2

Barlett, Donald L., and James B. Steele. *America: What Went Wrong?* Andrews and McMeel Publishing, 1992.

Barlett, Donald L., and James B. Steele. "The Really Unfair Tax" [online]. [Cited October 10, 2005]. *Time,* January 27, 2003. <www.time.com/time/magazine/printout/0,8816,411439,00.html>.

Brandt, Barbara. *Whole Life Economics.* New Society Publishers, 1995.

Center on Budget and Policy Priorities and Economic Policy Institute. "Pulling Apart: A State-by-State Analysis of Income Trends" [online]. [Cited April 20, 2004]. Press release and report on state income inequality, April 2002. <www.cbpp.org/1-18-00sfp.htm>.

Center on Budget and Policy Priorities. "EITC Outreach Kit." 2003. Current kit is available online <www.cbpp.org/eic2005/index.html>.

Citizens for Tax Justice. "Statement of Robert S. McIntyre, Director, Citizens for Tax Justice Before the House Committee on the Budget Regarding Unnecessary Business Subsidies." Transcript of statement. June 30, 1999.

Citizens for Tax Justice. "Most of House GOP Tax Plan Would Benefit Best-Off Five Percent" [online]. [Cited October 10, 2004]. Press release, May 6, 2003. <www.ctj.org/pdf/thom 0503.pdf>.

Government Accountability Office. "Tax Administration: Comparison of the Reported Tax Liabilities of Foreign and U.S.-Controlled Corporations, 1996–2000" [online]. [Cited October 15, 2004]. <www.gao.gov/new.items/d04358.pdf>.

Herman, Edward. *The Federal Budget: A Guide to Process and Principal Publications.* Pierian Press, 1991.

Institute on Taxation and Economic Policy. "Bush Policies Drive Surge in Corporate Tax Freeloading" [online]. [Cited December 4, 2004]. Report, September 22, 2004. <www.ctj.org/corpfed04pr.pdf>.

Johnson, Nicholas, Bob Zahradnik, and Joseph Llobrera. "State Income Tax Burdens on Low-Income Families in 2002" [online]. [Cited June 30, 2004]. Report for Center on Budget and Policy Priorities, April 2003. <www.cbpp. org/4-11-03sfp.htm>.

McIntyre, Robert J. *Hidden Tax Entitlements* [online]. [Cited June 20, 2004]. Report for Citizens for Tax Justice, 1996. <www.ctj.org/hid_ent/contents/ content.htm>.

McIntyre, Robert J. "Tax and Fend" [online]. [Cited September 20, 2004]. *Washington Monthly Online,* January/February 2003. <www.washington-monthly.com/>.

Network. *Learning About Taxes: Toward a Just and Fair System.* Report from Network: A National Catholic Social Justice Lobby, 1997.

Smith, Gar. "The Noble American Tradition of Tax Resistance" [online]. [Cited October 20, 2004]. Article posted on AlterNet, April 7, 2003. <www.alternet. org/story/15576>.

Thorndike, Joseph J. "The Price of Civilization: Taxation in Depression and War, 1933–1945" [online]. [Cited October 1, 2004]. An in-depth study of American taxation during the Great Depression and World War I, 2003. <www.taxhistory.org>.

United States Government. *Budget of the United States Government, Fiscal Year 2005.* US Government Printing Office, 2004.

United States Government. "Estimates of Total Income Tax Expenditures," Table 19-1 of Analytical Perspectives. In *Budget of the United States Government, Fiscal Year 2006.* US Government Printing Office, 2005.

United States Tax Code On-Line. <www.fourmilab.ch/ustax/ ustax.html>.

Wetterau, Bruce. *Congressional Quarterly's Desk Reference on the Federal Budget.* Congressional Quarterly, 1998.

Wilson, Edmund. *The Cold War and the Income Tax.* Farrar, Straus & Giroux, 1963.

Chapter 3

Center on Budget and Policy Priorities. *The Safety Net Delivers: The Effects of Government Benefit Programs in Reducing Poverty* [online]. [Cited June 5, 2004]. Report, November 15, 1996. <www.cbpp.org/SAFETY.htm>.

Collender, Stanley. *The Guide to the Federal Budget: Fiscal Year 2000.* Century Foundation Press, 1999.

Council for a Livable World. "Congress Should Reject Additional Military Funding" [online]. [Cited September 10, 2004]. Fact sheet, June 10, 2001. <http://64.177. 207.201/pages/8_22.html>.

Dobbs, Michael. "US Had Key Role in Iraq Buildup: Trade in Chemical Arms Allowed Despite Their Use on Iranians, Kurds." *The Washington Post.* December 20, 2002.

Grizzard, Buddy. "Estimate $3.3 trillion Missing from US Treasury" [online]. [Cited July 6,2004]. <www.heartcom.org/budget.htm>.

Indian Trust: Cobell v. Norton [online]. [Cited March 22, 2005]. Website with comprehensive information on Eloise Cobell's suit, n.d. <www.indiantrust.com/>.

Nader, Ralph. "Testimony Before the Committee on the Budget US House of Representatives" [online]. [Cited September 4, 2004]. Public Citizen, June 30, 1999. <www.nader.org/releases/63099.html>.

National Priorities Project. "On Budget, Off Budget Federal Spending" [online]. [Cited June 10, 2004]. Budget pages, updated December 2003. <www.national priorities.org/budget/budgetpages/OnOffBudget.html>.

Pember, Mary Annette. "Huge Accounting Scandal Must Not be Ignored." *The Progressive Magazine*. December 11, 2002. Available online <www.progressive.org/Media%20Project%202/mppd1102.html>.

Springer, John. "Broad Cuts in Entitlement Programs Under House Budget Plan." Center on Budget and Policy Priorities report. March 21, 2003.

US Department of Housing and Urban Development, Office of Community Planning and Development. Community Development Block Grant fact sheet, 1999, p. 2. Available online <www.co.san-bernardino.ca.us/ecd/pdfs/CommDevWeb/25th%20CDBG%20Anniversary%20Facts.pdf>

Weiner, Tim. "Pentagon Defied Laws and Misused Funds, Panel Reports." *New York Times*. July 22, 1999.

Chapter 4

Anderson, Marion. *Neither Jobs Nor Security*. Employment Research Associates, 1982.

Bureau of the Public Debt Online. "Frequently Asked Questions About the Debt" [online]. [Cited August 10, 2004]. Department of the Treasury, online questions and answers. Last updated November 3, 2004. <www.publicdebt.treas.gov/opd/opdfaq.htm>.

Eisner, Robert. *How Real is the Deficit?* Free Press, 1986.

Eisner, Robert. *The Great Deficit Scares: The Federal Budget, Trade and Social Security*. Century Foundation Press, 1997.

FedStats. "Economic and Financial Data for the United States" [online]. [Cited June 21, 2004]. US economic data, updated twice daily. <www.fedstats.gov/imf/>.

Financial Management Service [online]. [Cited March 22, 2005]. Home page of the FMS, which is a bureau of the US Department of the Treasury that provides the daily Treasury Bulletin and other governmental financial information. <www. fms.treas.gov/>.

Heilbroner, Robert L., and Lester C. Thurow. *Economics Explained*. Simon & Schuster, 1982.

Kennedy, Magrit. *Interest and Inflation-Free Money*. Permaculture Institute Publications, 1988.

OMB Watch. "The Budget Surplus Comes from Cuts in Discretionary Spending" [online]. [Cited April 20, 2004]. Article on OMB Watch website, July 7, 1999. <www.ombwatch.org/budget/1999/surplus.html>.

Orszag, Peter, and Robert Greenstein. "Federal Debt: What Matters and Why" [online]. [Cited June 20, 2004]. Report for the Center on Budget and Policy Priorities, February 22, 1999. <www.cbpp.org/debt.pdf>.

Shaviro, Daniel. *Do Deficits Matter?* University of Chicago Press, 1997.

United States Government. *The Citizens Guide to the Federal Budget* [online]. [Cited January 10, 2004]. 2003 Guide and earlier years available at <www.gpoaccess.gov/usbudget/citizensguide.html>.

Chapter 5

Architect of the Capitol. "The Statue of Freedom" [online]. [Cited October 10, 2004]. Description of the history and characteristics of the statue. <www.aoc.gov/cc/art/freedom.cfm>.

Atkins, Scott Eric. "The Pilgrims in the Capitol" [online]. [Cited October 15, 2004]. Part of a work completed for the Capitol Project, from the American Studies group at the University of Virginia. <http://xroads.virginia.edu/~CAP/puritan/purrot.html>.

Budget and Accounting Act of 1921 (P.L. 67-13; 42 Stat. 20-27).

Center for Responsive Politics. "2004 Election: Incumbent Advantage" [online]. [Cited March 22, 2005]. Fact sheet, n.d. <www.opensecrets.org/overview/incumbs.asp?cycle=2004>.

Center for Responsive Politics. "Financial Services: Top Industries Giving to Committee Members" [online]. [Cited March 22, 2005]. Information on donations from 2004, n.d. <www.opensecrets.org/cmteprofiles/indus.asp?cycle=2004&CmteID=H05&Cmte=HFIN&CongNo=108&Chamber=H>.

Center for Voting and Democracy. "Under-representation in the U.S." [online]. [Cited October 15, 2004]. A section of "The Feminist Case for PR," July 15, 2004. <www.fairvote.com/women/case_underrepresentation.htm>.

Congressional Research Service. "The Committee System in the US Congress." Report #95-591 GOV, May 10, 1995.

Congressional Research Service. "Congress: Sources of Legislative Proposals." Report #96-663 GOV, August 2, 1996.

Domhoff, G. William. *The Power Elite and the State: How Policy is Made in America*. Aldine, 1998.

Domhoff, G. William, and Richard L. Zemiegenhoff. *Diversity in the Power Elite: Have Women and Minorities Reached the Top?* Yale University Press, 1998.

Greider, William. *One World Ready or Not.* Simon & Schuster, 1997.

Guinier, Lani. "Making Every Vote Count" [online]. [Cited October 20, 2004]. Posted on the Miners Canary website (a version of the article first appeared in *The Nation* magazine), n.d. <www.minerscanary.org/mainart/every_vote_count.shtml>.

House Committee on the Budget. "Basics of the Budget Process: A Briefing Paper" [online]. [Cited November 30, 2004]. House Budget Committee website, February 2001. <www.house.gov/ budget/budget-process-brf.pdf>.

National Voting Rights Institute. "Seeking A Fair Democratic Process: The Ohio 2004 Recount" [online]. [Cited December 10, 2004]. Update on NVRI efforts, n.d. <www.nvri.org/about/ohio_recount.shtml>.

Robinson, Randall. *The Debt: What America Owes to Blacks.* Plume Books, 2001. (See also www.randallrobinson.com/debtexc.html).

Chapter 6

AFL-CIO. "It's Time for Working Women to Earn Equal Pay" [online]. [Cited March 20, 2005]. Section of AFL-CIO website with data and action regarding pay equity, n.d. <www.aflcio.org/issuespolitics/women/equalpay/>.

Coalition of Labor Union Women. "Pay Equity" [online]. [Cited March 20, 2005]. CLUW information and programs for pay equity, January 26, 2005. <www.cluw.org/programspayequity.html>.

Elson, Diane. "Gender-Neutral, Gender-Blind, or Gender-Sensitive Budgets? Changing the Conceptual Framework to Include Women's Empowerment and the Economy of Care" (report prepared as part of the Preparatory Country Mission to Integrate Gender into National Budgetary Policies and Procedures). Commonwealth Secretariat, 1996.

Greider, William. *Secrets of the Temple: How the Federal Reserve Runs the Country.* Simon & Schuster, 1989.

Henderson, Nell. "Unemployment Rate Falls to 5.7%; Employers Added Just 1,000 New Jobs in December." *The Washington Post.* January 9, 2004.

OMB Watch. "States Struggle to Fund Medicaid" [online]. [Cited March 23, 2005]. Fact sheet using figures from the National Conference of State Legislatures, August 11, 2003. <www.ombwatch.org/article/articlview/1721/1/91?TopicID=1>.

United Kingdom, Office of National Statistics. "Time and Use Data in the Household Satellite Account: October 2000" [online]. [Cited December 10, 2004]. Report on economic impact of unpaid work, October 2000. <www. statistics.gov.uk/articles/economic_trends/Household_Satellite_Account_Time _Use_Data_Oct2000.pdf>.

Waring, Marilyn. *Counting for Nothing: What Men Value and What Women are Worth.* University of Toronto Press, 1999.

"Wealth." *Encarta Encyclopedia* [CD Rom]. Microsoft, 2000.

Wolff, Edward. "The Wealth Divide: The Growing Gap in the United States between the Rich and the Rest" [online]. [Cited March 23, 2005]. *Multinational Monitor* 24, no. 5, May 2003.<multinationalmonitor.org/mm2003/03may/may03interviewswolff.html>.

Chapter 7

Ambrose, Soren. "Activists Target IMF, World Bank on Their 60th Birthday" [online]. [Cited August 23, 2004]. In *Economic Justice News Online.* 7, no. 2, April 2004. <www.50years.org/cms/ejn/story/57>.

Budlender, Debbie. "Review of Gender Budget Initiatives." Report prepared for Community Agency for Social Enquiry (Johannesburg, South Africa), 1999. Available online <www.wiram.de/gendersourcebook/downloads/Gender BudgetsBudlender.pdf>.

Committee on National Statistics. "Designing Nonmarket Accounts for the United States: Interim Report" [online]. [Cited November 16, 2004]. Summary of a book published by National Academies Press, 2003. <http://books.nap.edu/books/NI000423/html/1.html#pagetop>.

Community Services Block Grant web page [online]. [Cited December 10, 2004]. Administered by the Office of Community Services, US Department of Health and Human Services, February 1, 2002. <www.acf.hhs.gov/programs/ocs/csbg/>.

Economic Policy Institute. "NAFTA at Seven: Impact on Workers in All Three Nations." EPI briefing paper, 2001. Available online <www.epinet.org/briefing papers/nafta01/nafta-at-7.pdf>.

Federal Reserve Board. *Statistics: Releases and Historical Data* [online]. [Cited August 25, 2004]. A list of all statistical releases from the Federal Reserve board of governors, n.d. <www.federalreserve.gov/releases/>.

George, Susan. "A Short History of Neo-Liberalism." Paper presented at the Conference on Economic Sovereignty in a Globalising World, March 24–26, 1999.

Jubilee 2000 Coalition. "Carrying the Burden" [online]. [Cited September 5, 2004]. Article on women and the debt crisis, n.d. <www.jubilee2000uk.org/jubilee2000/features/women0412.html>.

Kroft, Steve. "All in the Family" [online]. [Cited September 10, 2004]. Broadcast on *60 Minutes,* CBS News, September 2003. <www.cbsnews.com/stories/2003/04/25/ 60minutes/main551091.shtml>.

New Zealand, Office of Statistics. "New Zealand Time Use Survey, 1999" [online]. [November 30, 2004]. Article based on New Zealand's first time-use survey, April 2000. <www.stats.govt.nz/ products-and-services/Articles/timeusesurvey 1999.htm>.

Public Citizen. "World Trade Organization (WTO)" [online]. [Cited September 15, 2004]. Announcement of new book on WTO, 2004. <www.citizen.org/trade/wto/>.

Swirski, Barbara. "What is a Gender Audit?" [online]. [Cited September 10, 2004]. Report from the Adva Center, August 2002. <www.adva.org/genderbudgets english.htm>.

UN Department of Economic and Social Affairs, Economic and Social Development. "Economic Statistics" [online]. [Cited November 30, 2004]. Web index of international statistics, November 2004. <unstats.un.org/unsd/nationalaccount/default.htm>.

World Bank Group. "United States Data Profile" [online]. [Cited October 20, 2004]. Profile of economic indicators, August 2004. <devdata.worldbank.org/external/CPProfile.asp?SelectedCountry=USA&CCODE=USA&CNAME=United+States &PTYPE=CP>.

Chapter 8

Bartle, John, and Marilyn Marks Rubin. "Gender Budgeting: Looking Through a New Lens." *Public Administration Review* (forthcoming).

Cavanaugh, Cathy. "Aurora Online with Marilyn Waring" [online]. [Cited September 20, 2004]. Interview with the author of *Counting for Nothing: What Men Value and What Women are Worth,* January 1998. <http://aurora.icaap.org/talks/waring.htm# heading>.

International Budget Project. "The Participatory Budget Process in Brazil" [online]. [Cited March 28, 2005]. Transcript of workshop with Joao Sucupira and Leo Mello, February 24, 1999. <www.internationalbudget.org/conference/2nd/brazil.htm>.

Lewitt, David. "Porto Alegre's Budget Of, By, and For the People" [online]. [Cited March 28, 2005]. *YES! Magazine,* Winter 2003. <www.yes magazine.org/article.asp?ID=562>.

Zinn, Howard. *A People's History of the United States.* Harper Perennial, 1980.

Index

❖

ABOUT THE AUTHOR

❖

JANE MIDGLEY IS A LONG-TIME ADVOCATE for peace and justice. She began her organizing efforts in Washington, DC at the Washington Peace Center where she focused on the effects of militarism on women and youth and helped to organize national demonstrations on a range of social justice issues. Jane has also participated in coalition efforts for disarmament and women's rights, including mobilizing national organizations to oppose the deployment of the first-strike Cruise and Pershing II missiles in Europe and attending the 1995 United Nations Fourth World Conference on Women in China.

She has twenty five years' experience addressing the US national budget. She focused on budget policy as both legislative and executive director of the Women's International League for Peace and Freedom and has written and spoken extensively about budget priorities. Her study The Women's Budget, calling for a 50% cut in military spending and an investment of those resources into human needs was used as the basis for citizen hearings around the country.

She received her BA from Carleton College and was a fellow in Peace Studies at the Bunting Institute at Radcliffe. She currently directs Strategies for Success, working with nonprofits and executive directors. She lives in Somerville, MA.

If you have enjoyed *Women and the US Budget*, you might also enjoy other

BOOKS TO BUILD A NEW SOCIETY

Our books provide positive solutions for people who
want to make a difference. We specialize in:

**Environment and Justice • Conscientious Commerce
Sustainable Living • Ecological Design and Planning
Natural Building & Appropriate Technology • New Forestry
Educational and Parenting Resources • Nonviolence
Progressive Leadership • Resistance and Community**

For a full list of NSP's titles, please call **1-800-567-6772** *or check out our web site at:*

www.newsociety.com

NEW SOCIETY PUBLISHERS